Paige! I never met someone who throws shade as quickly as I do until I met you! Thank you for being such great friend! Started from DMV now we here!

First Printing, 2017

Editor: Domonique Lingad

ISBN 0692913076
ISBN 978-0692913079

BLOSSOM

Dezari Alexander

First Printing

For all the flowers that are struggling to blossom, keep going, keep growing, the light will come.

Blossom

DEZARI ALEXANDER

The Soil

Growth. Growth. When you think about growth, do you think about spring? Do you think about maturity? What does growth look like to you? Growth is the key to survival. If the trees didn't grow, we wouldn't have air and if the crops didn't grow, we wouldn't have food. Both are vital. Every single one of us was placed in this human form for a reason, and to discover that reason we must grow. We all have inner wounds, whether it is generational curses, childhood trauma, heartbreak, abuse, mental illness, or addiction. The wounds are really lessons and lessons are blessings in disguise. Think about it. Growth isn't pretty, easy, or glamorous.

It's the anxiety that whispers in your ear when you're in a good mood, it's the inability to get out the bed because your depression suffers you, it's chasing your next fix, it's getting involved with that person who you know isn't good for you, it's ugly. To grow we must look back and reflect. First you must locate the wound. After you find it, you're going to get the urge to run from it like you've been doing your entire life. Don't run. It's time to face it head on. Now that you've located the wound, open it up. Meaning acknowledge it and be vocal. This can be done with a therapist, by yourself, or with a close family member or friend. By being vocal and opening the wound, it makes it real, and I know that's scary. After its wide open you will feel exposed, you will feel vulnerable. Oh crap, here come the tears. Go ahead, cry, cry it out. Every flower needs water to grow. Next you will get your shovel and start digging. Yes, dig out the gunk, dig out the dirt, dig out the lies, dig out the betrayal, dig out the pain, and dig out the scar tissue. It hurts I know, but keep digging. You must get rid of anything that no longer serves you. Once you are done, it's time to stitch it close. You can't put a Band-Aid on it, you can't wish it away, and you can't pray that it'll close magically. YOU, yes you must stitch up the wound yourself! Well damn, how do we do that? Lace your stitching needle with an abundance of forgiveness, soak the stitching thread in self-love, and then place a seed of peace inside the wound. Now begin stitching. I know it stings, keep going. You thought digging was the most painful part of this growth process? No, stitching is the most difficult because it forces you to forgive those who've wronged you, it causes you to forgive yourself, and it eliminates the excuses you've given yourself as to why you haven't evolved. All stitched up? Ok perfect. The seed of peace that you've planted will begin to grow and cover you. Now you are ready. I'm giving you these instructions from my personal experience. My story isn't pretty but it's triumphant. I wrote this book to heal, I wrote this book for my future children, I wrote it for anyone who believes that they won't make it through the storm, I wrote it for you. This book has healed me in so many ways, and left me with a huge therapy bill ha! I hope my story helps you see the light; I hope it motivates you to keep going. Thank you for journeying with me. It's time to blossom.

"If we're going to heal, let it be glorious." -Warsan Shire

Petal 1

"I'm a pretty little ballerina! I'm a pretty little ballerina."
I sang as I skipped holding my mom's hand.

We were walking quickly through the Kennedy Manor apartments in Richmond, California. As my pink tutu bounced and my metallic wand danced in the air, I continued to sing. A woman stopped us.

"Alright now ballerina! You are so pretty!" she said.

I smiled ear-to-ear. "Thank you!" I responded.

It was Halloween and we were rushing to meet the rest of my cousins for trick or treating. I was the happiest little black ballerina in the world. At only three years old, I had no idea of how chaotic my life was. If you had asked me I would have said I was a princess waiting to move into my big castle.

We entered my mom's good friend Gia roach infested apartment and I instantly snapped out of my ballerina fairytale. The apartment reeked of old cooking oil and cigarette smoke. I skipped into Gia's daughter, Kayla's bedroom.

"Come on Kayla! Let's go trick or treating before it gets too dark!" I said as I tugged her arm.

We raced to the door and began laughing. Walking through Kennedy Manor with our pillowcases full of candy felt regal. Kayla and I were arguing about which one of us would eat the most candy, when we were blatantly interrupted by gunshots.

"POW! POW! POW!"

My mom India shouted, "Oh shit! Let's go, they shooting already!"

She frantically grabbed both of us and raced back to the apartment.

My three-year-old eyes perceived India as a goddess. She had chocolate skin, plump lips; almond shaped eyes, and wore a slicked back ponytail like Sade. She was perfect to me. Only thing slicker than her hair was her mouth. India didn't take any bullshit from anyone; she knew how to argue herself out of any situation.

We returned to Gia's apartment panting, out of breath. Kayla and I were ordered to go into her bedroom to play. As we were walking to the room I knew what was going to happen in the roach nest of a living room. Gia and India were both drug addicts. Alcohol, crack, weed, you name it they did it. Back then in the mid 1990's, it was the norm. Our low- income apartment that we called "*The Manor*" was full of addicts and gangsters. It wasn't a healthy environment, but it was a family, a community of people repeating detrimental cycles.

While in the living room, the only thing that mattered to Gia and India was the crack sitting in front of them. I started to sing to myself as I brushed my doll's hair; little did I know ignoring the hell and chaos around me would become a habit of mine.

My escape from The Manor was my grandparent's house. Ironically there was a quiet suburban area right around the corner from the hood. Going to my grandparent's house was the highlight of my day.

My grandpa was a tall, soft-spoken, lean, handsome man with a salt and pepper colored high top. He was a drummer and a handy man, which made him even more smooth and cool to me.

"Papa!!!" I screamed as I ran into his arms.

He swooped me up into his arms and took me into the kitchen. I ran directly to the breadbox where he kept his Safeway branded chocolate chip cookies. Eating those cookies was another way I kept myself distracted from the pandemonium. Their house was full of warmth and love, sprinkled with the sweet smell of potpourri. My nana was the complete opposite of Papa. She was a loud, thin, outspoken woman with a laugh that will make any day better. Nana walked into the kitchen with her smooth caramel skin, gold clip on earrings, and low cut curled hairstyle.

"My baby is here!" she exclaimed as she hugged me.

After the initial excitement of seeing them settled in, I ran upstairs to see my aunties. The sweet voice of Mary J. Blige was blasting through the radio as I stormed into their bathroom.

"Real love, I'm searching for a real love..."

The bathroom had a window in the shower that made me feel like I'd escaped to a tropical island. I looked through the window at the plum, apple, and pear trees in the backyard then danced into the bedroom. My aunties were everything to me. They both were tall, skinny, had soft eyes, relaxed hair, and bright smiles. Brooklyn, my eldest auntie was my favorite. I called her Tee because Brooklyn was too hard for me to pronounce. She was everything I wanted to be. She would paint her lips with red lipstick and occasionally wear chunky braids in her hair, looking like the beautiful women in the 90's videos. My other auntie, Paris was wild, carefree, and rebellious. She had long nails, a long ponytail, with a body laced with silver bohemian jewelry, gorgeous. Paris was more like my nana while Tee was more like my grandpa. They both smothered me with hugs and kisses as I came into the room. They made me feel special and loved in every way. I adored them both and wished I could stay with them forever. As I sat and played in their makeup, I had no idea how quickly that wish would come true.

Petal 2

Corte Madera was the go to place for shopping, eating, and enjoying good weather. There was a thriving outdoor mall with an upscale atmosphere, and of course we didn't fit in at all. We headed to the end of the mall, where Nordstrom was located. The sun was shining on my freshly greased scalp; I wore a white t-shirt, and blue jeans. India, my great aunt Gloria, and I entered the store and headed to the women's section. I was four years old, still tiny as a button, and curious as ever. Aunt Gloria was nana's younger sister, and just as sassy as nana was. She had smooth caramel, honey-scented skin; long candy apple red nails, high cheekbones, and perfectly arched eyebrows. I begged India to take me to a toy store; she assured me that we would go after they finished shopping.

Aunt Gloria and India both began ruffling through the racks of clothes, picking out bold garments with lace and bedazzled accessories. I played in between the racks and entertained myself. After they were done picking out the clothes, we headed to the fitting room. The three of us went into the biggest stall and India directed me over to the bench. She began layering me with clothes, adult sized clothes.

"Mom, these clothes are too big for me." I said.

"We are playing dress up; you gotta put these clothes on to win the dress up game." She responded.

After she layered me with the clothes, she put a huge red hooded sweatshirt over the top half of my body and a pair of huge red sweatpants over my legs. I didn't know this back then but the red sweat suit was meant to disguise the layers of clothes underneath. I looked in the mirror and laughed. I looked like a giant red balloon.

"I look like Santa Claus! Did I win the dress up game?" I asked.

"Yes, you won, now let's go." She said as she grabbed my hand.

Before we left the dressing room, Aunt Gloria put some of the clothes in her huge purse, and India placed the rest of them in a wrinkled Nordstrom bag. We walked out of the fitting room and headed to the door to leave. I was walking slower than usual due to all the clothes I had on, I felt weighed down. Nonetheless, I thought it was hilarious and fun. I was smiling and laughing on our way to the door, singing Christmas songs, pretending I was Santa Claus. India kept telling me to lower my voice and walk faster.

As soon as we walked out of the door, we were ambushed. Two white men and a white woman ran up to us, guns drawn.

"Drop the bags, drop the bags! Put your hands up now!" yelled the white woman.

Aunt Gloria complied, while India began to argue with the woman. The woman placed India in handcuffs and one of the men did the same with Gloria. Everything in that moment began to move very slowly, I felt like it was a bad dream. I stood there trying not to scream, but then I began to cry. My heart was racing, my head began to throb, I was so afraid. After cuffing India, the woman came over to me. She told me that everything would be ok, and then she proceeded to remove the layers of clothes from my tiny body. After she was done, I was back in my white t-shirt and jeans. I cried for my mom as the men took her and Gloria away. The woman stayed with me until my mom's boyfriend Jeffery got there to pick me up.

Jeffery was a big, heavyset man, full beard, and brown skin. On the outside, he appeared intimidating but he was as gentle as a feather. He was like superman to me. Whatever we needed he got it for us. When he arrived, I ran to him and cried even more. The entire car ride, I continued to re-play what had just happened in my mind. I was devastated that the men took my mom away; I didn't say a word the rest of that day. Jeffery dropped me off at Yaya's apartment and later that day nana came and got me. Yaya was nana's mother and the matriarch of the family; she was the glue that kept everything together.

Months later I barely noticed that I had moved into my grandparents' house. I was enjoying being in a stable home. My wish to stay with my aunties had come true. I continued to ask about India and when she was coming back. They told me that she was on this great vacation and that she would be back soon. I asked them why didn't she take me on the vacation, I was told that it was a grown-up vacation. Ultimately, I stopped asking after a while.

One night I overheard Tee talking on the phone about how India was in jail and how bad of a mother she was. I was shocked, hurt, and confused. *How dare she leave without saying bye? Is she ever going to come back?* I thought to myself. These questions rushed through my young mind.

The next morning, I convinced my nana to take me with her to The Manor. She was going on her daily visit to see Yaya and she allowed me to come along. As we walked through Kennedy high school, nana and I sung.

> *"Ain't there something I can give you, in exchange for everything you give to me, read my mind and make me feel just fine, when I think my peace of mind is out of reach."*

We loved Anita Baker.

We arrived at Yaya's house and I raced up the stairs. Nana nestled into Yaya's couch, began her weekly gossip with her siblings and I managed to squirm out of the apartment without being noticed. I ran to the apartment where my mom and I had lived, I wanted to see if she was back or if she had kept the window unlocked for me to get my toys. As I got to the front door I saw a piece of paper with "EVICTION" written on it. I didn't know what the paper said, so I went around to the side to see if the window was unlocked, it wasn't. Anxiety and panic rushed over me. I began knocking on the window frantically.

"Mom! India! Mom! Please open the door!" I screamed.

When I didn't get a response, I started to cry. I knew in my heart that India had to be back from her vacation. I sat there and cried until I got a headache. I picked myself up and walked back to Yaya's house. During the walk, I bombarded myself with questions, trying to figure out where my mom was.

I arrived back at Yaya's, no one noticed I was gone. Yaya poured me a bowl of her famous clam chowder and the questions in my mind ceased. I believe that Yaya knew I was upset, she always knew without me having to say a word. Her way of mending the hurt was food.

There were random people that would come over to Yaya's place to buy candy, Icees, chips, and even drugs. I would see them purchase small bags of strange textured substances; I thought it was candy in a special pouch. Like I said before, it was a community of people repeating detrimental cycles. When you immerse yourself in chaos you become a part of it. Yaya always told me that I would be the one. I didn't know what she meant by it, but I do now. *If you feel that you are the one called to break your family's generational curses, please know that you have a unit of angels guiding you every step of the way. Keep going.*

I played at the park with my cousins until it was time to go, then I returned to utopia with nana.

Petal 3

India did get out of jail and surprisingly she came to get me from my grandparent's house. She arrived with Jeffery and he loaded all the bags of clothes that I had accumulated into the car. I was happy when she finally came to get me, but a part of me was angry as well. I was angry with her for leaving me.

Jeffery was like my second father. My real dad name was Eric and he was in my life as well. I would go see him occasionally on weekends and on his off days. He was like my best friend; I would have so much fun with him. India wouldn't allow me to live with my dad full time; therefore, I relied on Jeffery to be the prominent male figure in my life. Jeffrey had other women besides my mom, so he couldn't provide us with a place to stay. Since we couldn't go back to the apartment in The Manor, we moved from couch to couch. One night we would sleep on Yaya's couch, the next night on a friend's couch, or our cousin Tasha's couch. I would wake up often in the middle of the night on one of those random couches and every time I did, my mom was gone. She would slip out in the middle of the night to prostitute for money or get high with Gia. Whenever I did wake up and noticed that she wasn't there I would cry until I fell back asleep. It wasn't an ideal living situation at all, but it was my new normal. *Feeling neglected by a parent can lead to finding yourself in unhealthy relationships, always looking for someone to be there for you. You have to save you; you have to be there for yourself.*

Around this time, I was almost five years old and I had developed a deep knowledge of the street life. I could tell you the name of any drug, how it makes you feel, and how much it costs. I was very quiet, shy, and my desires for being a princess were fading. Princesses don't sleep on beer stained couches, princesses have their own beds, and they live comfortably. I would look in the mirror and see a pretty chocolate girl, with a big smile, curly hair, and almond shaped eyes like my mom. But even though I perceived myself as pretty as a princess, I knew that my life was far from a fairytale. My castle wasn't coming; it was time to let that dream go.

After moving from couch to couch, we began to stay with our cousin Tasha. I would get nervous and anxious when it was time to eat and go to bed. I dreaded dinnertime because Tasha usually forced me to eat things I did not like. Bedtime was awful because I knew India wouldn't be there when I woke up. One night while staying at Tasha's house, India managed to leave earlier than bedtime. I thought it was weird but I didn't say anything and continued to watch TV with Tasha's two kids, Sophia and Darin.

My cousin Darin was a few years older than I was and he constantly found new ways to pick on me. He wasn't always nice to me but he was very protective over me. Any boy that would give me any issues had to answer to Darin.

That night when India left early, Tasha cooked spaghetti for us, I hate spaghetti. She yelled at me and tried to force me to eat it. Being the stubborn child I was, I refused to take a bite and sat there until she rushed me off to bed. When I woke up that morning, I noticed five huge orange trash bags in the living room. I looked through them and saw all my clothes. I instantly started balling my eyes out because I knew that meant I had to stay there. India had snuck my clothes into that living room while I was sleep. I also knew that I wouldn't see her for a while. She had left me again; I was devastated.

Darin and I often played with the neighborhood kids and our bond as cousins got stronger. He was like the big brother I never had. One day, we were playing in the backyard and he suggested a new game.

"You want to see something?" asked Darin.

Being the inquisitive child I was, I nodded yes. He grabbed my hand and we went to the side of the house. He looked around and checked to see if anyone was coming. He then pulled down his pants and looked at me with an evil grin.

"Ew! You are nasty, pull up your pants before I tell yo mama!" I yelled. I started to walk away but he grabbed my arm tightly preventing me from moving any further. "Let me go before I tell!" I screamed.

He grabbed my arm and demanded me to shut up. I was crippled with fear; I did not move another inch. I watched this person that I adored and looked up to transform into something wicked, right before my eyes.

"You see this?" he said as he pointed to his penis. I

nodded as tears formed in my eyes. "Ok, put it in your mouth." He demanded.

My stomach dropped, I was so scared that I almost pissed my pants. My palms got sweaty, my face felt like it was on fire, and I wanted to run away. As I attempted to run, he pulled my arm forcing me to the ground. I knew this wasn't right but I was so scared and did not want Darin to get any angrier. So, I did as I was told. My arm throbbed with pain and tears continued running down my cheeks. Darin was someone I trusted and I couldn't believe he was making me do this. I could not help but think of how angry I was with my mom for leaving me here at this awful house, full of horrible people. This torture lasted for what felt like hours. After he got what he wanted, he pushed me back to the ground and stood over me.

"You bet not tell anybody, you hear me? If you do, I'll keep punching you." he said as he zipped up his pants.

I stayed on the ground crying. I hated everything about Tasha's house; I wanted to run away to my grandparent's house. I tried to call Jeffrey several times but there was no answer. I wanted to tell someone about what Darin did but I was afraid. I was a child that believed that I did something wrong. I placed the memory deep down inside me, suppressing it with everything I had. I wanted this nightmare to be over but it was only getting started.

Petal 4

After the incident with Darin I became even more quiet and to myself. I felt like every adult around me had let me down and no one was there to protect me. I stopped playing outside with him and stayed in the house most of the time. I had no desire to play with any of the kids.

I lived at Tasha's house for a few more weeks until India and Jeffrey came and picked me up. It was the summer before I began first grade. Jeffrey had an old-school Cadillac that screamed "hood rich" but I loved it. It was a limo in my eyes. The seats were cream color leather, the exterior was candy apple red, and it was scented with the new car smell.

While riding in his car, I would picture myself living in the castle I dreamed of, with a huge crown on my head, smiling and waving to the people of the village. That car gave me back my dreams of being a princess. *The angels that protect you will give you a beacon of hope to keep you going, to keep you on track to your destiny.*

Jeffrey stopped the car in front of brown dirty apartment building and I snapped out of my daydream. His placed a huge smile on his face and India was blushing ear-to-ear.

"India got her ownnn place! India got her ownnn place" he sang and danced as he came to open my door.

I climbed out the car confused and excited at the same time. As I walked up the stairs to our new place, I got happier and happier which each step I climbed. I thought this was going to be a new beginning for us.

The apartment was in San Pablo near the city library. India often referred to it as "Little Tijuana" due to the number of Hispanics in the area. The houses were colorful, the streets smelled like tortillas and fried corn; it was definitely a lively neighborhood. Our apartment was quaint and small. It had two bedrooms, one bathroom, and a cozy little kitchen. If I was to look at the apartment today, I wouldn't even consider it as a potential but back then it was grand. The view from the kitchen window was of a huge lemon tree, I loved it.

I finally had my own bedroom, but I insisted on sleeping with India. Sleeping with her was the only way I was sure she wouldn't sneak out in the middle of the night. I used my bedroom as a playroom and an escape from India's loud gatherings.

One day, she had some friends over and they were smoking weed. Of course, I knew the smell and cost of the weed, but I didn't know how it made a person feel. After her friends were passed out on the couch, I began to nag her with questions about it.

"Mom can I try it? I want to be like you. Let me try it pleaseee!" I begged as she lit her next blunt.

She began to laugh, shrugged her shoulders and

mumbled, "Anything to get you to shut the hell up."

She inhaled and coughed slightly before handing it to me. I had no idea what to do so I mimicked exactly what she did. I felt my stomach turning in circles and something told me not to do it but I did it anyway. I inhaled and allowed the smoke to travel down my lungs. I exhaled quickly and waited for something drastic to happen. It didn't.

"Mom let me try again." I whined.

India handed it back to me and I repeated what I did the first time. This time I began to choke. Tears ran down my face and I struggled to catch my breath. I ran into the kitchen to get some juice. My mom began laughing. I guzzled down the two cups of juice, grabbed the cookie dough out of the refrigerator and went into my room. I felt dizzy and tired. I didn't laugh or dance around like I thought I would. I just wanted to go to bed. *Children aspire to be like their parents despite their flaws, be mindful of the example you are setting for your children. We are working to break the curse, not to continue feeding it.*

All the time spent moving from couch to couch and the haunted memory of Darin resulted in me waking up in the middle of the night crying most nights. I was terrified every time I woke up in the middle of the night but I'm not sure what I feared exactly. It was the beginning of a long battle with anxiety. *When you feel the anxiety arrive in your body, try to dissect it, try to get to the root of it. It's usually our higher selves trying to communicate with us.*

If I were sleeping in India's bed, she would shut me up by giving me candy. She didn't hold me or tell me everything would be okay. She would shove candy in my face.

Like the cookies at my grandparent's house, candy became a numbing tool. That became my nightly ritual.

Eventually I began to make friends in our new apartment building. My first friend was a Hispanic girl named Vanessa. She and I were the same age. She was beautiful with long, wavy hair that flowed with the wind. Every time we would get together I would play with her hair. I wanted my hair to be like Vanessa's. I inquired about her hair and how she got it to be so perfect. Her mom pointed to the television and told me that she used the product shown on the screen for Vanessa's hair. The commercial was an advertisement for L'Oréal Kid's hair conditioner. I hugged Vanessa goodbye and wished her family a good night. Her mother attempted to teach me Spanish, so I danced out of the apartment yelling "Buenos Noches!"

I raced next door to our apartment and asked India to buy me the same condition that Vanessa used. She laughed and flicked my ponytails.

"Girl, you are not Mexican! That conditioner is not going to change your hair. It will still be curly." She said.

I started crying and begging her to buy it anyway because I still had hope of it changing my hair. The next day we walked to the corner store and bought it. I smiled the entire way home. This was it; I was getting a chance to be someone new. After getting my hair washed that night, I ran to the mirror to see my "new" hair. To my disappointment, it was still a curly Afro. I sat on the toilet and cried until India yelled and told me to go to bed. *When we go through rough situations, we tend to look at other people lives and maybe even try to mimic what they do. We want to know why their lives seem to be better than ours. Comparison is a kryptonite, it poisons your self-esteem.*

India continued to have numerous gatherings at the apartment. She rarely cooked so I began to binge on all things sugar, and she didn't bat an eye. As long as I let her get high in peace, she was fine. She stopped bathing me nightly; I began to wear the same outfit over and over again. I was still very young so of course I didn't care at all. One day India woke me up telling me we had to go to court. After her arrest in Corte Madera, she continued to get in trouble with the law. I heard her on the phone with nana saying something about a warrant. I had no clue what it meant.

"I'm going to take your granddaughter with me to court so the judge will see that I can't go to jail today. Can you give us a ride?" India asked nana on the phone.

"Fine, fine, we will walk!" she shouted before hanging up the phone.

India put my shoes on and wiped the sleep out of my eyes, as she called it.

"Mom my tutu itches, I need to wipe." I said.

"I'll give you a bath when we get back." She said as she put my jacket on.

I didn't know it back then but my body was rebelling against all the sugar I was eating. I had my very first yeast infection and it was extremely uncomfortable. The walk to the courthouse was rough. I kept stopping to scratch my private parts, and began to whine about my feet hurting. India dragged me along, she was adamant about making me appear in court with her. She needed me to be her get out of jail free card. The more we walked, the more I itched and ached. The walk was fifty minutes long. It was damn near an hour of walking with shoes that were too small and an itchy tutu. It was pure hell.

By the time we got to the courthouse, I knew something was really wrong. I removed one shoe and noticed four blisters on my toes. They were red, swollen, full of puss, and warm to the touch. I wanted to cry but I held in it. India's plan to bring me to avoid jail time worked like a charm. The judge allowed her to leave and she was ecstatic. I couldn't walk another fifty minutes back home; my feet felt like they were on fire. We got to the corner and I showed my mom the blisters on my toes. There were now ten blisters, one on each toe. She smacked her lips with frustration.

"I didn't know you needed new shoes, let me call nana to pick us up." She said.

"My tutu still hurts and it itches mom." I said as she picked me up.

"Ok we'll get you some medicine." She responded.

We walked over to the payphone and nana agreed to come pick us up. When we got home Aunt Gloria came over to give me a bath. She washed me up, teaching me the importance of washing every part of my body, especially my neck. She believed that a woman's neck should always smell good. My family was full of flawed people but the women all seemed to gravitate towards me to teach me a lesson or two. I'm not sure if it was because of the type of mother I had or if they were just God sent. It may have been both. *Take notice of the people in your life that attempt to teach you some things, listen, and receive it.*

That weekend I went to visit my dad and he noticed my blisters. I've never seen him so angry and upset. He stormed over to the phone to call India. They argued for a few minutes before hanging up. My dad was nothing like India. He had multiple jobs, worked hard, and made sure to give India money for me. Unfortunately, most of that money went to drugs and alcohol. They met before anyone knew how bad India's drug problem was. She was extremely smart, straight A student, could've had a very bright future, but unfortunately, she fell victim to temporary pain relief and artificial happiness. *There may be times when you feel like the wrong turns or detours in life may suffocate your aspirations and keep you down, and they will but only if you allow them to. You are always in control of your own destiny despite the detours; remember that.*

My dad had brown skin and a big smile. He wore a low fade haircut; he was just fly. Women loved him because they said he reminded them of Caine from the movie Menace to Society. After taking me the doctor for my blisters, my dad bought me several new pairs of shoes. He told me to make sure I wore them to avoid getting any more blisters.

We got in his car and he blasted his music as loud as he could and I swear they could've heard us across the world. He dropped off my new shoes and I back at home with India. My dad always came through for me.

Petal 5

It was a hot summer day in San Pablo. Vanessa and I sat on the porch eating popsicles, laughing at each other's jokes. We decided to walk around the corner after we were done eating. When we got back, we noticed a huge U-Haul truck at the house next door. There was a Hispanic family moving their things in. As we stopped to watch the family move in, a boy greeted us; he was around our age. When I first saw him I immediately thought he was cute. I was still five years old, so I didn't really pay attention to boys, but I definitely noticed him.

"Hi my name is Daniel. Who are you?" he asked in his Hispanic accent.

Vanessa wasn't shy at all; she gave him both of our names and told him that we would come over to play tomorrow.

The next day we did exactly that. We had a great time playing tag, hide and seek, and some board games with Daniel and his brothers. His brother Manny was eight years old and his oldest brother Jose was thirteen. Going over to their house to play became a part of our daily routine. Daniel and I would separate from the group and go to the library to read or walk to get candy from the corner store. We spent a lot of time together and we both liked the same things.

One day Vanessa wasn't home, so I went over to Daniel's house by myself. I knocked on the outside gate and Jose opened the door.

"Is Daniel here?" I asked.

"He went to the store, he'll be back. You can come in.," he said.

I was so excited for Daniel to come home because I wanted to show him a new book at the library. I was just one month away from starting first grade but I already knew how to read. The librarian, Ms. Mary taught me how to recognize and sound out words. My mom spent most of her days sleeping in until 3:00 p.m. and she barely noticed I was gone. The library made me fascinated with learning, I was looking forward to starting the first grade.

I walked into Daniel's house and sat down on the couch next to their birdcage. They had a beautiful yellow bird that I loved playing with. As I sat admiring the bird, Jose joined me on the couch. Their living room was a nice size with wood paneling on the walls, bright orange couches, and nearly every corner had a painting of the Virgin Mary. Both of their parents worked, therefore they were home alone most of the day.

"So, you starting school soon huh?" Jose asked.

"Yep, I'm going to the school around the corner."

He scooted closer to me and began asking me questions about Daniel. I answered them without hesitation because everyone in the neighborhood knew Daniel and I were inseparable.

"Do you touch yourself in the shower?" he asked.

I responded nervously, "No Jose, I wash up two times and get out."

He placed his hand on my leg. I was wearing a skirt and my favorite plastic sunflower backpack. I moved his hand and stood up quickly.

"I'm going to leave now, tell Daniel to knock on my door when he gets home." I said as I tried to hurry to the door. Jose pulled me back down on the couch and attempted to kiss me on my lips. I shook my head side to side preventing his lips from touching mine. "Get off me! I'm going to tell your mom! Get off now!" I screamed.

He began laughing and pulled my skirt up. I started to scream and kick while tears formed in my eyes. As I screamed and fought to get him off me, the bird began chirping louder. I began to scream India's name but our apartment building was too far for her to hear me. Jose starting rubbing on my butt, and I managed to kick him as hard as I could in his leg. That did not stop him at all.

He kept laughing and repeating, "I know you want this."

He pulled my underwear down and pinned me down with one arm. He then slipped his finger in and out of my vagina. It was extremely painful and I immediately yelled out in pain. He stood up and pulled down his pants. I pulled my underwear up in lightning speed. The pain gave me the strength I needed to get the hell out of there. I kicked him as hard as I could and dug my fingers into his eyes. I took off my sunflower backpack and raced to the door. Jose was right behind me. I swung the sunflower backpack and the zipper ran across his red face. I kept swinging the backpack and hitting him until he dropped to the floor. I ran out of the door and sprinted to my house. I opened the door and stopped to catch my breath. I began to cry again and tried to process what had happened. I looked at my backpack, and at that moment I began to associate sunflowers with protection. I looked at them as my saviors. The sunflower was there when no one else was there to help and protect me.

India came out of her room and began yelling at me. "Where have you been? Nana is on her way to get us!" she shouted.

"Mom I was at Daniel house and his brother..." she immediately cut me off.

"I don't want to hear it! Put on your backpack and get ready to go!" she yelled.

She went into the bathroom and I went into the kitchen. I starred outside the window and I pictured myself in the castle being the princess I desired to be. I wanted to run away, I didn't understand why people hurt each other. I heard India telling me to get ready again, so I pulled myself up off the chair. I wiped my face, washed my hands, and put my backpack on. On the bright side, I was getting to see my beautiful nana and I had my sunflower there to protect me.

Petal 6

Every Saturday morning, I would put on my swimsuit, pull out my beach chair, and sit in front of the television. I would eat my cereal and watch my favorite cartoons. At the moment, I would imagine that I was at the beach. I would even put on my sunglasses. My beach fantasies were often interrupted by India making me go with her to the corner store. There she would talk to the Hispanic and Black men that hung out in front of the store. After she talked to them, we would go back home and I would go into my room and lock my door. After the incident with Jose, I was terrified of males. Jeffrey stopped coming around, which meant our primary source of income stopped. India was desperate for money to support her habit so she began to prostitute. I knew that one of the men from the corner store was coming over. India and the man would go into her room for about forty-five minutes. After they were done doing whatever they did, she would immediately go into the bathroom and wash her hands. After I heard the front door close, I would go back to living my beach fantasy. India would then leave to go get some groceries from the store with the money she collected from one of the men. That became the weekend routine.

Vanessa would insist on us going to Daniel house every time we would play outside. I declined and eventually stopped playing with her all together. I avoided them at all costs. I missed Daniel, but I refused to step foot in his house ever again. I was afraid of his brother and didn't want to be put in that situation ever again. I buried the memory of Jose attacking me deep down just like I did the memory of the incident with Darin. I wanted a normal childhood free of anxiety, free of sexual abuse.

I became good friends with a boy I met at the library during a book signing. His name was Chance and even though I corrected him numerous times, he insisted on calling me "Girl" instead of my actual name. Chance had a weird accent that was foreign to me. He added more "S's" to his words and swayed his hips like the women in the music videos. He was my very first gay male friend. He liked the same things that I liked which were Barbie's, boy bands, and princess gowns. He was the sweetest person that I had met in that neighborhood. We would walk down the street swaying our hips and twirling like queens. We had so much fun together. An elderly couple adopted him when he was a baby and they were just as nice as he was. I would go over their house often for dinner and to watch cable. We didn't have cable so I would watch my favorite shows at their house. One day Chance and I were racing to my apartment and ran into a gorgeous, tall, curvy woman. She was coming out of my apartment and smiled as she passed us.

"Who is that girl?" Chance asked.

Ignoring his question, I watched the woman walk

down the stairs. I was in awe; she was lovely and I wanted to follow her.

"I don't know. Maybe she was looking for somebody." I replied.

"Well girl I'm going home to eat, you want to come or stay here?" he asked.

"I'm going to stay here, save me some cake." I said as I hugged him goodbye.

I walked into the apartment with the beautiful woman plastered in my mind.

"Mom! Who was that lady?" I screamed to India.

"That's my friend Cookie." India said as she walked into the living room.

"Is she coming back?"

"Yes, she'll be back later tonight."

I was so anxious to see Cookie again. I showered, fixed my ponytails, and put on my cherry flavored lip-gloss. I put on my pajamas with the matching slippers. I wanted to impress Cookie. She came back with two people later that night. One was her boyfriend Kevin and the other was her friend Frosty. Kevin was a tall, buff, black man with a nice face. I kept my distance from him. He was very nice to me and was constantly on the phone. Frosty was a curvy, bleach blonde white woman. She often wore light blue-colored skirts, dresses and silver lipstick. The three of them came with their luggage; they had planned on staying a while.

Every night before I was sent to bed, I would watch my mom apply the two women make-up. She would curl their hair, spray them with perfume, and fill their purses with colorful round small packages. After they were all dolled up Kevin would give them their itinerary for the night.

"Ok Cookie meet him at the motel 6, he likes black girls so you are on your own for this one." Said Kevin.

After receiving their duties for the night, Frosty and Cookie would both hug and kiss me goodbye and tell me how they wished I could come with them. They left the scent of cheap perfume on my pajamas and red lipstick marks on my brown cheeks. My curious, inquisitive mind began to wonder about their job occupation.

What did they do? Why did they come home from work so late? Why did Kevin take their money in the morning? I thought to myself.

I convinced Chance to help me find out what these two women did for a living. One day I took one of the colorful packages from Frosty's purse. We went to play with who we called the "trailer park kids" that afternoon. They were the kids that lived in the trailers across the street from my apartment building. My mom would warn me not to play with the trailer park kids, but I didn't listen.

Most of the kids left and went home, while Chance and I continued to play with another girl by the name of Lizzie. She was a white girl around the age of seven, with brown hair, green eyes, and splattered freckles on her face.

The three of us ran to the back of my apartment building and I pulled out the colorful package. "Look at this ya'll, this is what Frosty and Cookie be taking with them to work." I explained.

I then opened the package and seen a beige colored, round, latex object. Lizzie started laughing, "A Condom! Ew!" she exclaimed.

She then explained what a condom was to us and why people need them. Chance and I were shocked. I was upset that these two women would want me to come with them to their "jobs". The three of us sat in a circle starring at the condom, poking it with a stick, until we were interrupted by the neighborhood nuisance Jacob. He stormed over to us, and I quickly grabbed the condom.

"What are you hiding behind your back?"

"Nothing you trailer trash, get away from us." I snapped back.

He pinned me to the ground and ripped the condom from my hand. "Ew, you are nasty. I'm telling India that you are out here playing with nasty stuff!" he taunted.

I immediately knew that I would be in trouble if India found out but it didn't faze me.

To my surprise, Jacob did tell my mom about the condom and she was pissed. She took me into the backyard and asked me how I got the condom. When I told her how I got it she didn't believe me and slapped me directly in my mouth. I cried and ran into our apartment, anger consumed me. The next day India apologized and allowed me to ride my new bike. It was a hot pink Spice Girls bike that my dad had bought for me, I was so happy. I rode that bike everywhere. Chance had a bike as well and we would go far, far away from our neighborhood. With a mom like India and parents that were too old to care, we got away with it. I was racing Chance home from the store and my front tire hit a crack in the sidewalk. I flew off my bike and my left arm cracked in the middle when I hit the pavement. Chance panicked and picked me up off the ground, I was yelling out in pain. He rushed me over to my apartment building yelling for my mom.

India raced down the stairs and called the ambulance. She was so attentive and gentle. It was my first time seeing this side of her. The doctor wasn't able to put a cast on my arm that night so he sent us home and told us to return the next day. That night, I was in awe of this new version of my mom. She put me in the bed and made sure I had everything I needed. I woke up a couple of hours after she put me in bed, crying due to the pain of my newly broken arm. It was intolerable. I went into the living room to ask my mom for help. She was getting high with Frosty and Cookie.

"Mom my arm hurts really bad, I can't sleep." I whimpered.

"Go back to bed, you will be ok. I am busy." She snapped.

The sweet, caring, gentle woman that she was earlier that day was nowhere to be found. My feelings were crushed, and I was in so much physical pain.

"Mom, please." I cried.

India shoved a Reece's Cup in my face and demanded that I go back to bed. I walked slowly to the bedroom and cried the entire night. My arm was in excruciating pain. I ate the candy and continued to cry. Candy was India's way of shutting me up; it became my go to when I couldn't sleep or when I got sad. The sadness would come and leave quickly after I had some form of sugar. *The candy could have turned into something stronger as I aged. This exemplifies the importance of opening wounds and cleaning them out. When trauma isn't healed, and addressed, it will manifest itself, disguised as everything you've ever wished for.*

Cookie and Frosty moved out after a huge fight they had with Kevin over money. He insisted that they didn't turn in all their money one night, so he threw Cookie against the bedroom window shattering it. After they moved out, money became an issue again and India spiraled. She was accustomed to the money flowing in and supporting her habit. Once the money ceased, she didn't know how to deal with it.

Petal 7

I was now in the first grade, I enjoyed every minute of school. Everything they taught us, I picked up on very quickly; it came naturally to me. It was a struggle at first to write with a broken arm, but I managed to do it. My school was right around the corner from our apartment, so I walked there and back. Usually when I came home from school India was there and if she wasn't my auntie Paris was.

One day India left and asked a lady that lived across the street in the trailer parks to watch me. I was busy playing outside with Chance and realized it had gotten dark. Chance went home and I went inside the apartment. The lady that was supposed to watch me, came over made me food then left. I ate and went to bed. When I woke up the next morning, India still wasn't there. I ate the last of the cereal for breakfast then watched some cartoons. I began to worry and called my nana. There was no answer. I called back several times and still no an-swer. Nightfall came again and I ate cookie dough for din-ner. I was worried about my mom. I calmed myself down and went to bed. I woke up the next morning and decided to call my dad's mom, Janet.

"Hello?" she answered.

"Hi grandma, can you come get me?"

"Dez-mon? Where are you?" she asked con-cerned. That was her nickname for me.

"I'm at home."

"Let me speak to your mom."

"She…she's not here." I said quietly.

"Where is she?"

"I don't know. I haven't seen her in almost two days."

"What!!! I'm on the way, pack some clothes, I'll beep the horn when I'm outside." She said before hanging up.

My grandma came fifteen minutes later and my sunflower backpack and I was off to grandma's house. My grandma Janet was my complexion, smooth and chocolate, she wore a good amount of gold jewelry, and wore her hair in a blonde jerry curl. She was regal to me. When I arrived at grandma's house my cousins Michelle and Brandy greeted me. They were my dad's sister, Naomi's daughters. Michelle was my favorite cousin; we were one year apart in age and spent every moment fighting then making up and playing Barbie's. Brandy was a few years older than me and she let me get away with any and every-thing. I loved them both dearly, they were more than my cousins; we were like sisters.

My dad lived with my grandma at the time and she pulled him into the room to let him know what happened. I'm not sure how he reacted but I'm sure he was upset. Shortly after I settled in, India called my grandma's house. My grandma handed me the phone. India began yelling at me for calling my grandma. I tried to explain to her that I was hungry and she wasn't there for two days. She didn't want to hear it. She demanded that my grandma bring me back home. I was so sad when I had to leave my cousins.

When I got back home, my mom was extremely mad but of course that anger went away after she smoked and drank.

I continued walking by myself to and from school; I was fine until it was time to walk past Daniel's house. I was always scared that Jose would come out and hurt me again. To avoid that anxiety and fear, I began taking the long way to and from school.

I came home from school one day and found my auntie Paris and India fighting. They both were screaming and throwing things at each other.

"Bitch!!" yelled India as she threw the house phone at Paris's head.

Paris ducked then picked up the phone to call the police. Shortly after, the police were at our apartment, and they hauled India off to jail. I sat there and watched my mom being taken away from me again. It was just as hurtful as every other time, the pain was consistent, and it never got easier. *There will be times when we will be ripped away the people and places that are toxic to us. We may not realize the blessing in it at first but I guarantee when you look back; you will realize that it was your salvation.*

My grandma, Janet came to pick me up that night and this time it was for good. That was the last straw for my dad. He'd had enough of India's foolishness, he knew he had to step up and take custody of me, and he did. I was so happy to move in with my grandma and dad. I couldn't believe how my luck had changed instantly. *If you didn't get soaking wet and freeze during the storm, how would you know how to appreciate the warmth and sunshine? Your struggles aren't in vain, there is a method to the madness, there is beauty within your pain, find it.*

Petal 8

Grandma was so full of grace, humor, and love. She had a laugh that would tickle you to the core and a home decorated with silver and gold metallic décor. There was a huge mural painted on her kitchen wall, the carpet was soft and gray, and the rooms smelled like Avon skin so soft and floral plug ins. She had a closet full of flashy shoes and clothes. In her bedroom, there was a huge cabinet full of hygiene products. That cabinet was like a mini store. She had perfumes, a ton of nail polishes, Hawaiian Silky curl activator for her hair, Band-Aids, lotions, headache medicine, and anything we needed she had it.

My grandma taught me so much about being a woman and smelling like one as well. She taught my cousins and I how to paint our nails, dress appropriately for the weather, and she made sure we didn't leave the house without our hair combed. Every weekend my cousins Michelle and Brandy would come over. Grandma made sure her kitchen was loaded with sodas, oven bake pizzas, chips, cookies, and all things junk food related. We built forts made of expensive comforters, played with dolls, and argued until we drove grandma crazy.

My dad was funny and always had some type of jokes; he kept us laughing. He made sure I stayed on top of my homework and rewarded me with every report card. He was on and off with his high school sweetheart, Angela. She was a light toned, curvy, beautiful woman. She had a huge heart and sweet voice; she took on the role as my mother. See, while her and my dad were on a "break" he met India and then she had me. Angela was extremely hurt, but she got over it and eventually accepted me as her own. *Family is more than blood relations; it's the people who carry you through the dark when you are too heavy for yourself. Through this healing journey, you are going to need family.*

When I was two years old, Angela had a baby boy whom they named Cody. My brother was the spitting image of my dad, just lighter. Cody was full of energy, talkative, and one of my best friends. The four of us were a unit, despite the rocky relationship my dad and Angela had. The anxiety that was birthed while living with India began to fade away, and I was living life the way a child should. I was loved, healthy, and intelligent. The flow of my life was going well and everything seemed promising. *Sometimes the answer to your most complicated problems is to just surround yourself with people who love you. By changing your environment, you can change your life.*

Petal 9

My dad and Angela decided to move in together. The four of us moved into a nice condo in the hills. It was spacious, modern, and super clean. Angela was extremely neat and tidy; she was the prime example of how a woman should keep her house. Cody and I shared a room with bunk beds, a ton of toys, and a closet full of clothes. Some weekends our cousins would come over and we would go to the woods in the back of the condo. There were several steep hills and trees everywhere. It was serene; we made it our own personal playground. We would take huge pieces of cardboard, sit on it, and then slide down one of the hills until we reached the bot-tom. We loved the thrill. We named the different paths and rated them on their steepness. Whoever conquered the biggest hill, was the queen or king for that day. I hardly ever went down the big-gest hill, I was always afraid. *Problems and obstacles will arise but choose to align yourself with the solutions. Careful not to live in denial or convince yourself that everything is a cakewalk. Don't be afraid to figure things out, it builds character; it sows strength into your spirit.*

My seventh birthday was approaching and I was excited. I wanted every gift to be Pokémon related or money. India called my dad and asked him if I could spend my birthday weekend with her. She always called me around or on my birthday. I guess it was her way of convincing herself that she wasn't the world's most awful mom. My dad agreed to let me spend one night with her. I did not want to go with India, but my dad felt it was necessary. He was comfortable with it because India lived with Yaya in The Manor and he knew that she wouldn't allow anything to happen to me.

Friday arrived and I had my overnight bag packed, Angela double-checked the bag to make sure I had everything. My dad dropped me off at Yaya's place, we both walked to the top floor apartment, and I felt extremely anxious. I wanted to cry; my dad gave me a hug and assured me that everything would be okay. He told me to call him at any time and he would come get me if needed. I walked into the apartment and was welcomed with an abundance of love, hugs, and kisses from Yaya, my great aunts, and a couple of my cousins. My anxiety eased away and I felt much better. India came out of the room and greeted me excitedly. Later that day more family came over and it turned into a party. The apartment was flowing with laughter, loud voices, dominoes rivalries, endless cans of beer, and amazing food.

Once everything settled down I sat and watched cartoons. India left in the middle of the party and when she returned I could tell she was high. It didn't bother me because it's exactly what I expected. When it was time for bed, I made a pallet on the floor with Yaya's hand knitted quilts and a tower of pillows. I made sure to grab a few pieces of taffy from the candy jar on the glass coffee table and India came to lie down beside me. When I woke up the next morning, she wasn't there. Again, I wasn't surprised. I got up, folded the blankets, brushed my teeth, washed my face, and got dressed. After I got dressed Yaya woke up and made me breakfast. I ate and looked at the clock, it was 11:30 a.m. There was still no India in sight. I went to play in Yaya's makeup and perfume, and then asked her numerous questions about the different pictures on her bed-room walls. She had pictures of her children and most dated back to their high school days; they were all so beautiful.

"One day, your picture is going to be up there too." She said.

"Really? How old I gotta be to get a picture on the wall?" I asked.

"Well hopefully I make it to your graduation, and if I do we'll take a picture, and I'll put it right up there in the middle. It'll be the biggest picture too." She smiled.

Yaya was a special woman. Calm as a monk, but quick to snap at you if you stepped out of line. She took pride in her appearance, dressed to the nine, not a hair out of place. My mom's side of the family was full of imperfect people; addicts, prostitutes, men in and out of jail. She didn't care; she loved us all the same, never comparing one to the other, never judging. She tucked her sorrows and burdens away, painted her lips red, put a gold ring on nearly every finger, and carried on like she didn't have a care in the world. She managed to find peace in the middle of chaos. She could settle any argument with a look and make a four-course meal out of nothing, she was magic. Deep down I knew I was her favorite, maybe it's because I was her name sake or maybe it was the number of gifts I received at our Christmas gatherings compared to my cousins, or just maybe she was able to make us all feel like we were her favorite. I knew our connection was special; it was sacred.

"Grandmother, the alchemist you spun gold out of this hard life, conjured beauty from the things left behind, found healing where it did not live, discovered the antidote in your own kitchen, broke the curse with your own two hands."

−Warsan Shire

I got bored of playing in the perfume and makeup, so I washed my face, and went back in the living room. I watched a few shows and looked at the clock, it was now 2:45 p.m. and my mom still wasn't there. I got annoyed and thought, *this is exactly why I did not want to come!* I called my dad; I was ready to go home.

"Hey baby, how's it going?"

"It's ok. I'm ready for you to come get me." I replied.

"Why? Not having fun?" he asked concerned.

"My mom left last night and she still isn't here. I'm ready to go home." I said holding back the tears.

"Wow, okay. Let me put on some clothes and I'll be right there."

"Ok, bye." I said before I hung up the phone.

I sat and played with my Barbie's that Angela made sure I packed in my overnight bag. I put all my stuff by the door, preparing to leave. Another forty-five minutes passed and I called my dad again, but he didn't answer. India walked in and noticed my bags.

"Why is your stuff right here?" she asked hastily.

"I'm leaving; my dad is on the way." I said softly.

"What? I had a lot planned for your birthday week-end! Why are you leaving?" she yelled.

"You left, I didn't know if you were coming back."

India was angry, she stomped off into the bed-room, and I picked up the phone to call my dad. He answered, telling me he was on the way. Before I could respond, my mom snatched the phone from my ear.

"She ain't going nowhere! Stay at home, she is fine here!" she screamed.

I got scared and panicked. I screamed for my dad to come get me, I'm sure he heard me. India hung up the phone and went back into the room. She began to shuffle through things and I got up to wipe my face. When I walked out of the bathroom, I felt sharp object hit the left side of my face. I fell to the floor and began to cry again from the stinging pain. India was throwing the toys she bought for my birthday at me. One by one she threw them aggressively, making sure they hit me. After she ran out of toys to throw, she began to throw random objects, each ramming a different part of my body. I cried, screamed, and covered my head and face. My face ached with pain, my hands and arms were scratched up from the things being thrown at me, and I was terrified.

"You know what; go let Angela be your damn mom! I don't want you anyway! You hear me?" India yelled and walked towards me.

I continued to cover to head, I wasn't sure if she would try to hit me with something again.

"I hate you! I hate you! I bought all this shit and you

just gon leave? Fuck this! I hate you!" she yelled.

I froze; the tears began to feel like bricks run-ning down my face, I didn't want to believe that my mother had just told me that she hated me. That was the most painful thing I've ever experienced. My spirit instantly shattered into a mil-lion pieces.

I got up from the floor, grabbed my jacket, and looked out the window. I was in a state of hypnosis. I didn't under-stand what I did to make India not want me, I didn't under-stand why she treated me like I was worthless, I just didn't un-derstand. I also could not comprehend why Yaya didn't come help me, or why she allowed India to do this. I wanted to get away from everyone in that apartment. I placed my bag on my shoulder and walked outside. I sat on the bottom step and tried to calm myself down, rocking back and forth. The concrete stairs froze my tiny legs, so I stood up and grabbed a piece of the huge Aloe Vera plant that grew outside of Yaya's apartment and rubbed it on my face. I knew the plant would heal my wound from the impact of the toy. My dad pulled up and rushed over to me. He asked me what happened and I began to cry again. I couldn't talk at all. I got in the car and did not look back. I was done with India; I didn't want her as my mom anymore. She successfully broke my heart way before any boy had a chance to.

Petal 10

I decided after my seventh birthday to exile India from my thoughts, physical space, and life all together. I had a huge void in my heart from not having my mom. I ignored it; I did not want to linger on the sadness and emptiness. I did still have Angela, but no one or anything could replace my actual mom. Despite the disconnection from India, I had my auntie Brooklyn, aka Tee. She was adamant about being in my life. She would come get me on weekends or holidays. I spent plenty of time at her house and I adored every minute of it. She would take me to get smoothies and then we would binge on Mexican food. Our weekends consisted of trips to the zoo, horseback riding, and my favorite, going the aquarium. It was always an adventure with my Tee, she was well put together, straight to the point, and there for me. Anything I needed, Tee made sure I had it. She spoiled me rotten. I believe she tried to be there for me as much as possible due to India's absence. *Letting relationships fall where they fall can be one of the biggest pills to swallow. We tend to hold on longer than we should due to the intoxicating memories of how it used to be. They USED to be that way, leave the past in the past; you don't live there anymore.*

A few months after my dramatic seventh birthday, we received the news that Angela was pregnant. Cody, my dad, and I were all filled with excitement and joy. This new addition to our family was nothing short of a blessing. Cody and I argued about the sex of the new baby, we even placed bets on what it would be. I won the bet; it was a girl. I was looking forward to having a little sister and I couldn't wait until her arrival. My dad went into high gear after receiving the news that he was about to have a third child. He began testing for better jobs and received a good job offer.

In late December, Ella was born. She was a ten-pound bundle of joy and she was truly a blessing. When Angela and Ella arrived home from the hospital, I was in awe. I sat on the bed in my laundry-scented pajamas, and Angela placed Ella in my arms. She was sure to tell me not to drop her baby. We laughed and I promised not to. I sat and looked at Ella, she slept so peacefully. She began to wake up and cry. I got up and walked over to Angela, to give her the baby.

"She's crying because she doesn't like dark people, she only like light people like us." Cody snickered. Before I could get a response out of my mouth, Angela popped him and made him apologize. I laughed and we made up.

When Ella was around two years old my dad and Angela ended their relationship for good. My dad rented a tiny studio close to our elementary school, and the three of us began spending equal time with both parents. One week we would go with Angela and the next we would go to my dad's. The switching of weeks worked out perfectly.

My dad would wake us up for school in the morning

by blasting Snoop Dogg's "Tha Last Meal" album. Ella would wake up dancing, Cody would laugh, and I would sing along to the songs. "I don't carree what you do, long as you don't fuck with mine, you think you can't be toucchhedd…" I sang loudly thinking I was a rapper.

The studio was cramped but my dad sense of humor made it feel like a palace. Angela house was more structured, we had a set list of chores, had to be in bed by nine o'clock, and we always woke up in time for breakfast. Dad's house was more laid back.

The weekends were still spent with Michelle at grandma's house. Brandy was now a teenage and began having her own weekend plans. She didn't want to be bothered with her little sister and cousin. Brandy had a perfect smile, deep dimples, thick arched eyebrows, curly black hair, and eyes that could melt any heart. She was the calm medium between Michelle and me.

I was loud and always ready to argue with anyone despite his or her age. My mouth got me in trouble every time, but it didn't stop me from using it. I was acting out to distract myself from not having my mom around. Michelle was way more relaxed than I was but together we would get into everything. We would scare the shit out of people who were walking around the neighborhood, we would throw sunflower seeds at our sleeping uncle who lived with grandma, smoke papers with sage in the middle pretending it was weed, binge watched movies with grandma that weren't age appropriate at all, chased the ice cream truck down the hill; we had a ball.

Grandma's neighborhood was at the edge of Richmond; it was like its own little world. Big trees, steep hills, sunny skies, and calm breezes graced us every time we walked up to her doorstep. The neighbors acted as additional guardians, watching our every move when grandma wasn't paying attention. The hills were our secret hide away, nesting areas, and a place for Michelle and I plotted our next moves. Reciting movie lines was the nucleus of our conversations. My dialogue was quick and stumbled, while she spoke as calm and slow as a snail. She was the ying, I was the yang. We gave each house a name based on the people that lived there. There was the Voodoo man house, old man house, Asian house, and fine boy house. We made sure to walk slowly past the "fine boy house" and then looked at each other and quoted "How Stella Got Her Groove Back".

"I respect!" I would say.

"I re I re!" she would respond.

I couldn't imagine my childhood without Michelle she was my light. We knew everything about each other and made promises to always be there for one another. She had a red undertone, long reddish-brown hair, slightly slanted eyes, and gorgeous features. She had a sour patch kid demeanor (damn Gemini's), serene energy, would rather die than admit she was wrong, and always had a slick comeback. Michelle was an individual and everyone who encountered her was smitten. She was like honey.

My dad began dating a woman named Kerry and she came by the studio often. She had long, thick black hair, beauty marks on her face, and cookie dough brown skin. Kerry had three kids as well but we hardly seen them at first. When we did finally meet, them it was like meeting a long-lost cousin and we all clicked instantly. Her daughter Kia was the same age as Michelle, her oldest son Kaleb was Cody's age, and her youngest son Kyle was a couple of years older than Ella. Our ages collided perfectly.

Petal 11

It was the beginning of fall, around Halloween time. The mornings were breezy and crisp, and the afternoons were warm and toasty. Indian summer was coming to an end and Halloween was approaching. I had begun the sixth grade and my body started to develop. It seemed like everyone in my grade had went through some form of puberty that sum-mer. The boys were taller, the girls were more developed, and the teachers were afraid of the new hormones in their classrooms. I was experiencing the beginning of puberty. My height ceased, I traded my training bra for a real one, hips spread slightly, and booty got more round and poked outward. I wasn't shaped like a grown woman yet, but the changes were noticeable. My belly poked out due to my love affair with candy, but I was in awe of my new body. Angela was now working a second job and she bought most of our school clothes. I had every color velour sweat suit with the matching shoes and floppy hats. I was a mini Missy Elliot. I wore my hair in French braids and coated my 11-year-old lips with tons of sticky clear lipgloss. The boys at school noticed as well, the attention was foreign to me but welcomed. *There's hardly anything that can stop a woman who sips cups of poise chased with shots of confidence for breakfast.*

Michelle, Kia, and I decided to go to the movies to see the new horror movie "The Ring". The three of us were something like a girl group. Kia was tall, slim, and just as dramatic as I was. She loved eating, never gained a pound, had a "take no shit" attitude, and a big heart. She was fire with rebellion tattooed on her soul. She questioned everything, needed an explanation for parental demands, and pledged allegiance to her own flag. She was my sister.

It was Friday night and the three of us went to grandma's house and got ready for our first movie trip alone. Usually grandma insisted on accompanying us to the movies but she allowed us to go alone this time.

We got dressed in our skintight denim jeans, velour hooded jackets, huge hoop earrings, B2K spray painted shirts, and colorful knee high socks. We clearly followed every fashion trend that was popular back then in the early 2000's. At the movies, we seen familiar faces, guys who played football for the local pop warner league, girls from Kia's middle school, and a few of Michelle's friends. We sat in the theater laughing at jokes, eating sour straws, and drinking cherry flavored slushies. After the movie was over, we were terrified. The movie left an imprint in my mind, I was afraid to go to sleep that night and the following night. Kia and Michelle got over the fear of the fictional character; I however could not get it out of my thoughts.

The weekend was coming to an end and we returned home to get ready for the school week. We now lived in a run down, tiny, two-bedroom apartment located in the heart of the hood. My dad kept his humor and made us see the best in it. The carpet was dingy and brown, the bathroom could barely fit two people, the walls were off white with stains from previous tenants, and the scent of smoke flowed throughout.

Cody, Ella, and I slept in the first bedroom. We had makeshift bump beds, which, in reality, was one solid twin bed and a second twin bed on a rolling bed frame on the floor. The frame allowed us to push the bottom bed underneath the top bed when we wanted room to play. Ella and I slept on the top bed and I hated it. She had bladder issues, which resulted in me waking up numerous times covered in her urine. After the initial disgust and annoyance, I would wake her up, put her in the shower, change the bedding, and then clean myself up. When it was our week to stay at our dad's house I was her mom and had to do everything for her that should have been my dad's responsibility. He began spending his evenings drinking some type of alcohol and watching television after he would cook for us. I loved Ella, but I didn't love the burden of having to take care of her around the clock. My dad made it clear that she had to go everywhere I went. In the mornings, I would have to get he dressed first, brush her teeth, wash her face, comb her hair and make sure that she was fed. I felt like I was living the life of a teenage mother.

Ella had big brown eyes and chubby cheeks that made me melt. She was a life size doll with fair toned skin, curly hair, and features that resembled our brothers. Cody was still my partner in crime. He was now very outspoken and athletic. He would argue with everyone at school and would justify it by his desire to want to be a lawyer one day.

The movie, "The Ring" was still haunting me and I

woke up throughout the night terrified of the nightmares. One night Ella wanted to sleep in our dad's bed, terrified of sleeping in the bed without her, I went with her. That night I slept like a baby. No nightmares, no anxiety when waking up, no worries. We slept in our dad's bed that entire week. The last night we slept in his room, I had the strangest dream. I dreamt that someone was touching my breast, I tried to move the person's hands but they kept rubbing my breast. When I woke up that morning for school my bra was unsnapped and falling from my shoulders. I didn't have a clue what happened, I thought that I had slept too wild, and it had unsnapped by itself. I rushed into the bathroom and splashed water on my face. I took a deep breath, and pushed it to the back of my mind.

The weekend came and we went back to grandma's house but when we got home Sunday night, I told Ella that we would return to our own bed. I was still uneasy about the dream I had while we were sleeping in our dad's bed. We both adjusted quickly to sleeping back in our room. Ella and I would double team Cody, making him watch the shows we wanted to watch, making him be the guy voice for our male Barbie's, and just giving him hell. Like many siblings, we had moments consumed with petty arguments, but we all loved each other, we were a team. We didn't have much, but we had each other.

Petal 12

Spring came and I decided to follow in Michelle's footsteps and try out for cheerleading. I wasn't athletic at all, didn't have any rhythm, but I wanted to do it. The tryouts were brutal, I couldn't split my legs or jump as high as the other girls, but that entire week I worked my ass off trying to remember the choreography. After school, we would go to Angela's house and I would spend my entire afternoon and evening practicing in the mirror. I would practice at recess during school and would go to sleep counting 5, 6, 7, 8! All my hard work paid off and surprisingly I made the team. The coach was a handsome, flamboyant man, he felt bad for me and gave me a chance, I was ecstatic.

That enthusiasm halted when conditioning camp arrived. I had no clue what I had gotten myself into. We went to a local middle school and worked out nonstop for hours. The school was old but renovated, with a smell of tanbark, fresh paved walkways, and lilacs. The coaches would yell and scream as we ran numerous miles, jogged up hills, held water bottles over our heads, and did pushups and sit-ups. My body was in total shock, I was overweight, a junk food addict, and opposed to anything fitness. When we would run, my dad would yell "Don't finish last, run, run, don't come in last." That motivated me to run harder and faster. I was ex-tremely competitive and after a short amount of time I was running in front of every-one on my team, including the girls that ran track during the off season. The coaches began to take notice and compared the other girls to me. That didn't sit well with some of the girls, but I didn't care. Conditioning camp came to an end and I was twenty pounds lighter. At first I barely noticed to the changes in my body, everyone else did. Cheerleading became my life; I was happy to be a part of something and I loved my new body. *Having a healthy relationship with your body goes far beyond ex-ercise and proper diet, feed your soul some candy, sprinkle confetti on your emotions, balance is key.*

Cheerleading, school, and taking care of my sis-ter were a lot to deal with. I was exhausted after practice but that didn't matter, I still had to get everything in order for Ella. My dad began to drink more and more. People would praise him for being a black man that took care of his kids but, in reality, I was doing most of the work. One day I got Ella dressed in a red GAP hoodie and jeans. Ella was always tall for her age and she would grow out of clothes quickly. My dad didn't buy us clothes often so I worked with what we had. I rolled up her jeans to make them look like Capri pants. We left the house and the day continued as normal.

Cody and I went to Angela's house after school and waited for our dad, it was his week. My dad came to the door and I jumped up to give him a hug. I ran to the door and opened it. I reached out for a hug and instead I received numerous blows and slaps to the face and head. I started screaming and covered my face. Angela came to the door to see what the commotion was.

"Eric stop! Stop hitting her!" screamed Angela.

My dad continued to hit me until I fell to the floor and cradled myself into a fetal position. My face was stinging from the slaps and my head was pounding, I cried and Angela came and helped me up. I was petrified, I instantly flashed back to my seventh birthday.

"Do you see what my baby has on?" he asked angrily.

"Yes." I said whimpering.

"This damn hoodie is too small; her jeans are flooding! What the hell is wrong with you?" he yelled.

"Eric stop! You need to buy Ella more clothes! This is her sister not her child, she is your responsibility not Dez's!" she snapped at him.

My dad looked at me angrily and yelled for us to get our things and meet him downstairs. After that took place, I would get fidgety and anxious when I got Ella dressed for school in the morning, trying to make sure her outfits matched and everything fit. I would cry in the shower, wishing I were anywhere else but there. I couldn't comprehend why my dad got so upset. I eventually got over it but I never allowed myself to forget. *One incident, one action can change your perception of a person.*

Petal 13

My dad and Kerry relationship deepened. It was so serious that we blinked and before we knew it, Kerry and her three kids moved in with us. Six kids now occupied the tiny room with two twin beds; we were the black Brady brunch. I despised sharing my space with more kids, it was clutter everywhere. There were exactly three girls and the three boys. Cody, Ella, and I now had to share the top bed, and Kerry's kids were on the bottom bed. It was chaos. The number of toys and clothes in the closet tripled in size. There were fights over who drank the last of the milk, which would shower first, and who earned control over the television. To ensure that everyone got hot water, we had to cut the number of showers. Ella and I had to shower together, Kerry's two boys Kaleb and Kyle showered together, and Kia and Cody got the privilege of showering by themselves, individually. The more my body changed, the more I had the desire to shower and get dressed alone. I was forced to dry off and put on my pajamas in the tiny bathroom, while doing the same for Ella. It was a very tight squeeze but we adjusted.

Summer came and we were all ecstatic. We were free from homework, unjust daycare, and vexing bedtimes. We spent the summers having water fights, playing kick ball, and of course going to grandma house. Ella, Kia, and I would meet Michelle at grandma's house on Friday, and convince her to allow us to stay for the entire week, sometimes longer than the week. Grandma only allowed the girls to sleep over, she thought that the boys were too much for her to handle.

The three of us were obsessed with B2K, and would clean grandma's entire house for money to fuel our obsession. I was lazy and hated cleaning up, but anything to be able to buy every magazine, DVD, sun visor, t-shirt, and CD. I would purposely half clean everything so that grandma would deny me the right to clean certain sections of the house. I would sweep without mopping, rinse the dishes instead of washing them with soap, wipe off the bathroom counters leaving the toothpaste in the sink to dry alone, and I did it all with a huge mischievous smile on my face. I was the youngest, therefore she allowed me to get away with everything, and my cousins hated it. I literally almost burned the house down by micro-waving a potato for twenty minutes and grandma laughed it away. I could do no wrong in her eyes. I gave her bragging substance. My grades, my skin, and my daring attitude were fuel for her. She would boast about me to coworkers, neighbors, and anyone would listen.

The summer came to an end and I was now in middle school. I was excited about new friends, new clothes, and finally being able to switch classes.

One night Kerry and I made a huge batch of brownies. I always helped her in the kitchen. I wasn't eager to learn how to cook; I just loved being able to taste the food before any of the other kids. She was a wizard in the kitchen. Her enchiladas, pancakes, perfect fluffy eggs, golden brown fried chicken, tacos, and pastries all tasted amazing. She never measured, always went by what felt good, and made sure I followed her directions precisely. We bonded over her childhood stories, her lessons learned from past lovers, and her love for her grandmother. She was the executive cook, and I was her sous chef. Pour, mix, taste, listen, and repeat.

When the brownies were done, she gave us tiny pieces, and took the entire pan in the room with her and my dad. I was pissed, I spent the night helping her make them and I wasn't allowed a whole brownie. This night changed everything.

All the other kids were in the living room sleep in the fort they had built, Kerry was in my dad's room sleep, and I was in the bedroom alone watching my favorite movie at the time, Cheetah Girls. I was deep into the movie and thinking about all my aspirations just like the main character in the movie. I wanted to dance and be known for something bigger than myself. The movie made believe that it was possible. As I mentally accepted my Oscar for best actress, I noticed my dad standing in the doorway looking at me.

"Hey dad!"

"Hey baby, what are you watching?" he replied.

We talked about the movie and new things happening at school. He congratulated me on making the honor roll again and noticed my vague response. He asked me what was wrong, and I told him about Kerry giving us small pieces of the brownies. My teenage mood swings would not allow me to get over it. He defended her reasoning for it and he proceeded to come into the room. As he entered the room, I noticed the odor of alcohol coming from him. I was lying on my back, head was propped up with a pillow, and he sat next to me. We started joking about the fort the kids built in the living room and he teased me for having the bedroom wall covered in B2K posters.

The movie went on a commercial break and my dad began tugging on my oversized shirt that I wore to bed. I thought he was going to make a joke about me wearing the same shirt almost every night. Before I could get a word out of my mouth, my dad pulled up my shirt and I froze. My breasts were exposed; I instantly became nervous.

Confusion consumed my mind and I raised my hand to pull my shirt down. Before I could complete that task my dad began to kiss and lick my breast and nipple. I froze, my body was as still as a tombstone, I was in complete shock. My dad stopped and immediately pulled my shirt down and jumped off the bed. It was like a switch clicked.

"You want some brownies? I'm going to bring you some." He said quickly before he rushed out of the room.

I couldn't say anything, my body was paralyzed, and I wanted to jump out of my skin. Some minutes passed and I managed to get up. I jetted to the bathroom and began to scrub my breast with a towel, I wiped so hard that my nipple became raw and sore. I sat on the toilet and cried. I didn't know how to process what had taken place. I felt disgusting, I felt dirty; I felt violated. I sat on the toilet crying, rocking back and forth. I couldn't comprehend the fact that I was now gifted with not one but two parents that were utterly sick.

I pulled myself up and lethargically walked back to my room. There was a plate of brownies on the bed. Were the brownies supposed to make me suddenly get amnesia and forget about what had just happened? I put on a bra, another big shirt, and an oversized hoodie then got in the bed. I did not want my breast to be noticeable, so I covered them up as much as I could.

I felt so far away from my own body, I didn't want it anymore. I tried not to think about what my dad had done but my body refused to forget, it constantly reminded me of the incident. I would get a tremendous feeling of disconnect and severe disgust for many years, it was awful. If I wore anything that showed skin, the feeling would come rushing to me like a stallion of horses. *"I'm gonna look for my body yea, I'll be back like real soon."-Solange*

I thought about calling Michelle, but I didn't. I was embarrassed and distraught. My relationship with my dad was now tainted; it felt like my best friend had literally pierced my soul with a knife baptized in calamity. After that night, I got really quiet and I didn't talk as much anymore. I did not want to be noticed, I wanted to fade away. I thought that if I wasn't visible then no one could hurt me again. Kerry realized the change in my personality but my dad convinced her that I was becoming a teenage and that's what "teenagers do". He stopped letting me to go Angela's house during her week to have us, he told me that she didn't care about me, and therefore it was pointless. I don't believe I've ever felt so low, so worthless. I felt like that little girl again, I mentally pictured my old sunflower backpack, hoping it could save me now like it did then. *When you tote around a "family secret" it will melt your insides, choke your joy, and leave you with nothing but ashes. Speak what you feel, feel what you speak. Those are not your burdens to carry, return it to the person who gave it to you. Thanks, but no thanks; you can have this shit back.*

"What happens in this house stays in this house. What happens in my house stays in my house." He would say. I watched as people continued to worship my dad for being a "great single father" and it made me want to destroy everything in sight. However, I managed to successfully bury the secret deep down with the rest of my wounds. I carried on and pretended like everything was fine, like we were fine, but I was far from it. Now it was back to arguments over cereal and who gets to watch their favorite show. *Be cautious when placing someone on a pedestal the view will make their flaws appear obsolete.*

Petal 14

Cheerleading became my escape. It was exactly what I needed to keep going. It forced me to take back my voice. Each cheer had to be yelled loudly therefore the quiet facade I put up didn't work anymore. We would give each routine everything we had, leaving us panting for breath and crying over trophies. Our team was amazing, our coach made sure of that. We had early morning practices that ended in hill sprints or push-ups. It was tough, but it built us up. Young girls need to be reminded that they are magic, and performing at each competition did exactly that. I felt alive during each performance while my adrenaline raced through my body con-vincing me that I was capable of anything.

Middle school flew by and so did my cheer-leading career. I made genuine friendships during my time cheerleading. I became close with a brown, thick girl with soft features named Reyna. We spent a lot of time together battling childish break ups and baking everything in her mom's kitchen. Her mom didn't mind at all. She was a free spirited, youthful, vibrant woman. Reyna's mom and my dad became good friends and she would help us out a lot. Whether it was groceries, rides to school, or just offering kind words.

I was devastated when it was time to move on from cheerleading. It was something that sparked a passion inside me that I never knew I had. It felt like leaving home and going to a foreign country without a map or GPS. I had to suck it up and move on. It was now time for high school, whew where did the time go? My dad and Kerry ended their relationship and we moved again. The relationship between them two was over but Kia was still my sister, and we made sure to keep in touch.

The new house was close to my high school and Angela's new place. Ella and Cody continued to switch weeks and I was still stuck with my dad full time. Our house had three bedrooms and two bathrooms. Cody had his own room and Ella and I shared a room. All three of us shared the main bathroom and my dad had his own bathroom in his room. The house was dark, with a deep brown carpet, and smelled like cleaning products with a hint of cigarette smoke. It was across the street from an elementary school, surrounded with warm-hearted neighbors, and the house was always hot inside due to my dad leaving the heater on. I had a full-sized bed and Ella had a twin bed next to the closet. I kept all my toiletries on my dresser, a ton of teddy bears on the bed, and had pictures of my friends pinned to the mirrors. My room was always spotless; I developed an obsession with being clean. I saw it as something that I could control in my life. Most nights would be consumed with loud gatherings and parties hosted by my dad. He always had people over, mainly family and a few friends. His drinking didn't slow down and neither did my responsibilities for my siblings.

My freshman year of high school was the best year of my high school career. The school I went to was new, had a strict dress code, and dedicated teachers. The school buzzed with creativity, diversity, and was in the middle of the sunny suburbs. I took a lot of advanced classes in my hopes of getting into a good college. I thought college was my ticket out.

My desire to perform and dance was still instilled in me. I began choreographing dances with my friend Mario for the rallies. His style of dancing was more complex and technical while mine was the complete opposite, together we made the perfect team. I was beginning to be known as the girl from the rallies. After school, we would practice for hours with the sun beaming on us. We wanted to be the best, so we endured the smell of gravel that seeped into our senses and ignored the sweat sprinting down our faces. Practices weren't glamourous but it always paid off.

High school made ignoring sexual urges nearly impossible. I would talk to guys that were in their senior year, thinking I was too good for the boys my age. I would sneak on movie dates with them, make them bring me my favorite foods, and chill in their cologne scented cars after school. Everything would go smoothly until they suggested sex. My school was small and I didn't want to be labeled so I would cut them off. Sex wasn't a priority; it was something that I wanted to wait to do with someone I really cared about. *You are wonderfully made; however, you are not for everyone.*

Michelle and I lived close to one another and I spent most of my free time with her. We would scrap up any money we could find to keep our nails done and the rest would go to fast food and new clothes. Anything we did together was "fun", it could have been something as simple as going to the grocery store; we still had a ball. I had a great social life in high school, but I paid a price for it.

My dad began letting me go anywhere I liked as long as I checked in and answered my phone every time he called. I was happy with this freedom. I would go to parties, kickbacks, the mall, and to friend's houses. If there was something happening that weekend, I was there with Michelle or one of my friends. We stayed out, but my grades remained good. I was ambitious, had big dreams, and always had something to say.

Towards the end of freshman year, my bliss was abruptly interrupted. My dad continued to let me have my freedom but it was under one condition.

I would ask to go somewhere and he guilt trip me by saying that I didn't spend any time with him. The price I paid for going places was that I had to cuddle with him. It wasn't an innocent act; it was gravely inappropriate and perverse. I would have to lay with him, while he rubbed against me. I would get stiff as a board and try to keep myself from vomiting. That was a mistake, the stiffer I became the more he enjoyed it. I would stare at the white baseboards in the room, trying to imagine myself being anywhere but there. The smell of sweat stained sheets would drift into my senses and snap me back into reality.

"Yea, make it tight." He would repeatedly say.

It was the most uncomfortable thing I've ever had to do, besides the prior incident with him. The more he rubbed against and touched my body, the more excited he would get. It was atrocious; no child should ever have to experience the habitual act of someone using them as a vessel of impertinent pleasure. That was when the old feelings of disgust would come rushing back to me. When he was done getting what he wanted to get out of it, I would sprint out of that room. Immediately scurrying into the bathroom and wash my face to disguise the tears. After a while I stopped crying and the tears refused to come; I became numb. I kept quiet about it because I was still ashamed, still thinking it was something I could have done to avoid it. I started to hate my body again, blaming it for my dad's actions.

I would go to nana's house during all the breaks we got from school to get away. I would manage to stay at her house for a week until my dad would call demanding me to come home to clean up or something ridiculous. I knew his true motive and I would literally feel sick as I packed my clothes to go back home. My time spent with nana was always fun. We would go to farmer markets, flea markets, state fairs, and then return to her house to eat what-ever magic she created on her stove. It was the perfect distraction from the misery I had to endure at home. *Sometimes getting away from the chaos isn't a distrac-tion, it is a necessity; it is a survival tactic.*

Petal 15

The beginning of my sophomore year came down on me like a ton of bricks. My schoolwork doubled due to my class schedule but I managed to stay on top of it. I was depressed from my life at home and I was looking for an escape. I thought that my first boyfriend in high school Paul was just that. He was tall, nerdy, athletic, funny, and mysterious. He wasn't the type of guy that I usually went for but that's exactly why I liked him. He was different, his energy felt like honeycomb. He was extremely smart and would have a witty comeback to everything I said.

When I was with him, all my problems would perish. His hugs were therapeutic; he felt like my forever, like a savior. I convinced myself that I had to change for him to stay with me. I tried to be more poised, more reserved, more of someone else, and less of my actual self. I met his parents at one of his basketball games and they were lovely. His family was picture perfect and kind. Paul's dad was hilarious, always joking and making everyone around him smile. He was the biggest cheerleader for our relationship; he swore that Paul and I would get married one day. His mom was gentle and soft. She felt like the mother I'd always wanted. I confided in her about my relationship with my mom and she was shocked. I mistook her concern and care for pity and sympathy. Those made me stop talking about India and change the subject. I didn't want any pity for what I'd been through. I felt like it wasn't anyone's place to feel sorry for me, because I was still standing. I was shaking on a crumbling sheet of ice but I was still standing.

Ultimately, things didn't work out with Paul. I had to learn how to love myself and he needed to focus academically. The break up was brutal, but the chemistry between us never died. He was still a great friend to me and I always had him tucked away in my heart. The love was still there, but we both were young and had a ton of growing to do. *Be selfish with yourself; you belong to you and only you.*

The end of the sophomore year came and now it was summer again. I walked out of my dad's room and skipped the bathroom this time. He left out of the house. I felt sunken and lethargic. Being violated over and over again caught up to me. I looked at myself in the mirror and lost it. I threw a huge tantrum, knocked everything off my dresser and ripped all the pictures off my mirrors. I was full of rage and didn't want to live anymore.

"Dear God, please take me now. Please." I cried.

I sat and cried. I thought about ways to end my life, but couldn't decide. I took this as a sign that I was meant to keep going. I decided that if Paul couldn't save me or any other person for that matter then I had to save myself. I had to do something about it.

The next day, I finally built up the courage to tell Michelle. After I told her she was extremely upset and everything I didn't want her to feel, she felt. I didn't want anyone to hate or despise my dad because he was my dad and I loved him immensely. However, that love doesn't change what's right and what is wrong. After I told Michelle I thought I would feel better and I didn't. I felt exposed and still ashamed. She convinced me to let the shame go, assuring me that it wasn't my fault. That alone gave me the strength to make the most powerful move that I've ever made in my young life. *There will come a time when you must remove the shackles, axe away at the victim mentality, and place a survivor label on your chest.*

I was sitting on my bed full of nerves fidgeting with my nails. I picked up the phone and dialed my aunt Naomi's number, Michelle's mom. The numbers thumped as loud as a school bell as I dialed them. I got up to make sure the house was empty before I finished dialing the number. I pressed send and took a deep breath.

"Hello?" she said.

"Hey auntie, I have a question." I said fighting back the tears.

"Hey girl, what's up?" she asked.

My auntie and I shared the same complexion. She had long black hair, was fashion forward, perfect framed body after having five kids, and could turn heads without saying a single word. She was beautiful. She had a no-nonsense approach to most situations; this made me nervous.

"I…I wanted to ask you if I can come stay with you. I can't live with your brother anymore." I said nervously.

"He is a mess, right? Your grandma was the same exact way. I don't care you can come, just keep my house clean." She said.

She had no idea what I endured living with my dad, she thought I wanted to leave because he was strict and over bearing at times. I didn't care what she thought the reason was I was just happy that she said yes.

"Ok thank you so much. See you soon." I said before we hung up.

I called Michelle to tell her the good news and she came right over. When she arrived, we began frantically stuffing my clothes in garbage bags, placed my toiletries in plastic grocery bags, and erased any evidence that I lived in that room. We hauled the bags to her car, placed them in her trunk and back seat, then we drove away with-out saying a word. My heart fluttered, my palms began to sweat, and I felt like I was dreaming. Was this really happening? Was I finally getting away? It was real. *You are the hero that you've been waiting for.*

After I settled into my auntie Naomi's house, I knew it was one more thing that I had to do. I asked to borrow one of my auntie's cars and headed back to my dad's house. I walked in the house, slightly shaking, mentally telling myself to be brave. I went into my room first, making sure that we got everything that I needed, and then went into my dad's room. He was lying on the bed, watching T.V. I stood in the doorway, stopping myself from entering the room completely.

"I'm going to live with my auntie." I said calmly.

"What? No, you aren't. You think you can tell me what you gon do? You aren't grown!" he replied hastily.

"I can't live here anymore, I'm tired of taking care of

kids that aren't mine." I said as tears began falling from my eyes.

"You can't leave me, I need your help. You can't leave." He said quietly.

At that moment, everything that I've been suppressing burst wide open, I was full of rage. My face got as hot as lava and I felt like I was going to explode.

"Are you kidding me? I am done living here! I'm done being a maid; I'm done being touched by my damn dad! You think it's ok making me cuddle with you? You think it's ok? You need help, I'm done and I'm leaving!" I shouted.

My dad began to cry and looked away from me.

"Ok." He said softly.

I turned and walked to the front door. I got into the car and didn't look back. I was proud of myself, I was full of gratitude for having the opportunity to leave, and I finally felt free. It was liberating. I still wasn't over what my dad had done and I still despised him. My phone began to get flooded with calls and texts from family members asking me why I left. Everyone told me how wrong and ungrateful I was for leaving my dad's house after "everything" that he'd done for me. I didn't give a shit about anyone's opinion because they didn't know my truth. They were all running marathons with their assumptions. I didn't tell anyone about my real reasoning for leaving because I didn't want to face it; I wanted to be happy and live with my aunt and cousins. It wasn't worth it to me, so I left the wounds closed and untamed. I wanted to finish my last two years of high school without any more trauma fueled tears; I wanted to feel normal for once. *Affirm your peace, you are deserving of all things golden.*

My auntie's house was relaxed, no set time for eating, and no ridiculous rules. She let us do whatever we pleased if the house was clean. Michelle, Kia, and I began getting invited to eighteen and up parties. We would decorate our faces, get dressed in tight shorts or dresses, and thick heels. The parties were wild and harmonious. Music blasting from the speakers, eye candy in nearly every corner, and the three of us in the midst of it all. We'd return home in the late hours of the night, remove the shoes from our sore feet, wash the sweat off our bodies, and return to school Monday with a new story to tell. Life was good; we were young and carefree.

Petal 16

It was a perfect, sunny, warm California day, and my senior year of high school. I continued living with my auntie. Her neighborhood was full of cookie cutter, picture perfect houses that resembled homes from the set of a movie. Angela decided to move out of the state to help her mom and she took Ella with her. It broke my heart to see them go but I understood her reasoning.

Michelle and I decided to go to the Berkeley flea market, our go to place for body oils, black art, and jewelry. After we got dressed in our bright colored summer dresses, wedge heels, and oversized bohemian bags I ran to the mailbox. The mailman, Sam and I were now on first name basis, he knew I was waiting for my college acceptance letter. I greeted him and rushed over to our mailbox. Sam was grinning ear-to-ear, which made my stomach turn in circles; he knew something. I grabbed the mail and immediately saw a big white envelope with bold, red letters.

Michelle pulled the car around and waited for me to get in. "Hurry up girl, let's go!" she said.

I threw all the mail back into the mailbox and kept the big white envelope. I ripped the lining, and pulled out the stack of papers. Tears formed in my eyes and I began to scream.

"I got in!! Northridge wants me girl!" I screamed.

"Bittcchhhh you got in! Yes!" Michelle yelled.

She got out the car and we started dancing in the street thanking God, thanking the universe, and thanking ourselves. We hugged and got in the car. I couldn't believe this was manifesting. I thought that moving to southern California would bring me a ton of happiness. I felt a wave of gratitude rush over my body; I was glowing the entire day. However, I didn't know that with growth come lessons.

Graduation day came and I looked at myself in the mirror in awe. I managed to graduate with honors, was the poetry editor of my high school's literary magazine, won scholarships for college, and ready to take on the world; I was the ancestors dream. *During the flight of your life you will endure some turbulence, but I assure you that you will reach your destination.*

As a graduation, present Angela took me on my first cruise. This cruise was different because it was a black cruise. It was a boat full of educated, beautiful black people. The vacation was everything I expected it to be and more. Endless food, serene clear blue water, and some eye candy. I gravitated towards a group of people around my age and we clicked instantly. The days were spent on a beach drinking anything we could get our underage hands on, the nights were spent partying at one of the clubs on the boat or on the deck dancing the night away. The last day was full of long hugs, number exchanges, and promises to keep in touch.

After getting off the boat, we went back to the hotel in Miami. I settled in the lobby while my mom got the key to our room, I forgot all about my phone and pulled it out of my bag. I checked the CSUN portal to make sure everything was set for move in day for the dorms. I noticed that the university removed me from the dorms. I had to use my dad's income for my grants so he was the person of contact for the school.

He admitted to missing one call, which was the verification call for the dorms. I was livid; I felt like my dreams of having a typical college experience were being crushed.

I held back the tears as Angela walked over to me. She noticed something was wrong and demanded me to tell her. "It'll be okay, you just have to use your scholarship money to get an apartment. Everything will work out, what is meant for you is for you." She said to me.

The day that I had to leave for college, I was a nervous wreck. I was terrified to leave Michelle; she had been my support through everything. I knew I had to leave to grow, but it was one of the hardest things I've ever had to do.

The day I left for CSUN I still didn't have an apartment, financial aid was nowhere to be found, and I had to ride in the car with my dad for six hours. I was sad, angry, and anxious all at once. Before leaving I posted on a roommate site to find someone, anyone to live with. When we arrived to Northridge I checked my email and found a possible roommate. We decided to meet her and her mother at an apartment complex ten minutes away from campus. I sucked it up and accepted the roommate offer and the dingy apartment. We pulled up and I saw Cyn, she was around 5'4, peanut butter complexion, black spots on her face and arms, and singles in her hair. She was rough around the edges, her mother reminded me too much of India, and for some reason I didn't trust neither one of them but I needed a place to stay. *Your intuition is a direct link to your higher self, it sails you through this human experience, follow it.*

The first week of classes, I took the bus to cam-pus and back home. I hated everything about the bus; I wanted to live on campus. My friend from high school felt bad that I lived so far from campus and he introduced me to his cousin Rain. He knew she would be someone for me to hang out with. Rain and I were best friends from day one. She was 5'5, glowing smooth skin, long black hair, and freckles on her nose, with eyes as big as the moon, and the body of a track star. We had so much in common. We were both from the Bay Area, both virgins, both had mommy issues, and surprisingly we discovered that we were both on the same cruise. We didn't hang out on the cruise but we shared similar stories about the vacation.

Rain lived in an apartment directly across the street from the dorms, with two other girls Justice and Layla. After meeting her roommates, I started going to their apartment frequently. The first weekend at CSUN we all went to get piercings. I decided to get my tongue pierced and tried so hard to conceal it from Angela. She would call me every other day and I had to convince her that my voice was different due to a cold when it was the swelling from the piercing. We were eighteen, no parents, no rules, pure freedom.

Rain and I spent all our free time at the dorms meeting new people, attempting to do homework, and exploring the campus. The campus was beautiful and tranquil. There were huge trees, a lot of restaurants, a huge number of students from all walks of life, and a library that had an iconic set of stairs. One day I returned home from class to find Cyn and a man in our bedroom. We shared a room but had separate beds. She introduced me to the man and I told her to come in the living room. I asked her who he was and she became defensive. "I met him today at the mall." said Cyn.

I was beyond shocked that she brought a complete stranger into our home. Due to my fear of strange men, I packed some clothes and accepted Rain's invitation to sleep over at her house that night.

It was draining living with Cyn. She smoked in the house, masturbated loudly in the shower daily, and every time I came home she had a new stranger in the house. I was beyond uncomfortable and regretted my decision to move in with her. The breaking point was two months after living at the apartment. I came home and one of her friends was sleeping in my bed and another friend was in the kitchen cooking the food I had bought the day prior. I called Rain; she insisted that I move in with her and her roommates.

"They like you and I already asked them, it's fine just come." She said.

"Are you sure? It's going to be three girls in one room." I responded.

"Yes, I'm sure, we'll come get you in a few." She said before she hung up.

I packed all the things important to me, placed all my clothes in storage totes, and put everything by the door. I left my bed, the living room furniture, and the bathroom décor. I didn't want any of it, I felt like Cyn and her random friends had tainted it. I went to the leasing office and told the manager that I needed to break my lease. She warned me about the fees and before she could finish I took the last of my scholarship money out of my bag and placed it on her desk. She smiled and said "ok honey, good luck with everything."

I signed the papers and went back to finish packing. Rain arrived shortly; Justice and her cousin Jennifer accompanied her. They helped me take my belongings to the car and we were ready to take off. Cyn was on the phone with her mother, and tried handing the phone to me before I left. "What does she want?" I asked before taking the phone.

Before I could say anything Cyn's mother began yelling, threatening me to leave the apartment without taking anything that Cyn would need. Without hesitation, I threw the phone, flipped the coffee table over, and began to raise hell. The tone of her mother's voice set me off, I didn't have a mom to talk to me that way, and Cyn's mom wasn't going to neither. I was in a state of rage, everything began turning red, I snapped. Every memory of betrayal, neglect, and abuse raced into my mind. I began yelling and cursing unable to calm myself down. Rain rushed me outside and she placed me in the car.

"Calm down D, it's over. You don't have to deal with her shit anymore." She said.

I looked out of the window, my breath slowed down, and my heartbeat relaxed, I began to soothe myself.

"Sorry guys, I don't know what came over me." I said quietly.

"It's fine, we were ready to fight if they tried anything."

said Jennifer.

"Now we know who not to fuck with, you are insane girl." said Justice.

We all began to laugh and proceeded to make plans for the night. I was comfortable, I felt like these girls understood me. We went back to their apartment and I settled in.

My new living situation worked out perfectly. I had great friends and the energy in the house was harmonious. We would go to class Monday through Thursday, and have a three-day weekend. Rain got into a relationship with a guy from Inglewood named Jordan. He began to throw parties at his two-bedroom dorm and was adamant about getting me to meet his roommate Bryce. I didn't know anything about Bryce except that he was hardly at their dorm. I agreed to meet him that upcoming weekend.

When we first met, he sat on his bed and starred at me for a while. I looked away and he began to ask me questions about myself. We sat and talked for hours, not aware of the time. I looked outside and noticed it was dark.

"We've been talking all day, I'm about to go find Rain." I said to him.

"Ok, are you coming back?" he asked.

I blushed and giggled, "not tonight" I said as I walked out.

Over the course of that semester Bryce and I spent time together and I didn't know if his attraction to me was purely physical or not. He was very attractive, light shaded skin, hazel eyes, head full of curls, slanted eyes, and full lips. I had to compose myself every time I went around him. His birthday was approaching and he invited us to his party, which was going to be at his dorm.

Justice, Rain, and I took extra time to get ready for that party. I wore a tight floral corset, skinny jeans, and my comfy heels; I was clearly looking for attention that night. We all thought we looked like perfection and we headed to the party. We stopped at our friend Casey's dorm to pre-game. We guzzled shots of UV chased with gulps of Four Lokos. This was my first time relying on alcohol to relax me. We walked to Jordan and Bryce's dorm, alcohol in hand, vanilla scented skin, and loud laughs.

Everyone greeted us as we walked into the party and we passed around our drinks. We were drunk and ready for the party. The heat from all the bodies instantly hit me, it was packed, and I felt all the guys starring at us, but I was looking for Bryce. Rain went to find Jordan and Justice went to smoke on the patio. She had to smoke black n mild's when she drank.

I went to the bathroom, looked in the mirror with realized how blurry my vision was. I laughed to myself; I loved being drunk it made me feel invincible. I opened the bathroom door and Bryce was standing there, waiting for me.

"H...Hi." I said.

"Hey, where you been?" he asked.

"We just got here, we..." I attempted to say as he pulled me in for a kiss.

We moved into a corner away from the party and kissed again. It was impossible to control my drunken raging hormones at this point. He pulled away from me and put his head down.

"What's wrong?" I asked.

"I can't do this, sorry don't hate me" he responded.

Confusion plastered my face; I thought everything was going great between us. I inched away from him and posted on the opposite wall. He came closer to me.

"You are the type of girl guys want to marry, the keeper. We are freshmen in college; I want to enjoy my first year. I'm not ready for someone like you." He said as he attempted to pull me in for a hug.

I backed away, looked at him, grabbed my drink, and walked away. I was hurt but the alcohol didn't allow me to dwell on it in that moment. I continued to drink until I forgot about what Bryce said to me.

The rest of the night Rain and I danced with nearly every attractive guy in the room. We were drenched with sweat, having a ball. I went to the patio to get some air and locked eyes with a guy named Gary that I had met while trying to find one of my classes earlier in the semester. He was a senior; therefore, he knew the campus well.

Gary grabbed my phone from my hand and I tried to get it back but he held it in the air. My small arms couldn't reach his 6'2 frame.

"I'm putting my number in here, make sure you hit me up."

I laughed and snatched the phone away from him.

"Maybe."

He leaned in and whispered, "You will."

I smiled as he walked away, but was quickly interrupted by the voice of my nemesis Ryan.

"Bruh, I heard you got your tongue pierced! So, you a hoe now? Only hoes have tongue piercings." He snapped at me.

97

"Shut up Ryan! Fuck you, I can't be a virgin and hoeing at the same time."

"Yeah you better still be a virgin, saving it for me, right?"

"Absolutely not, hell no." I said as I pushed him out the way.

Ryan and I met one night when Rain dared me to take some beer from the refrigerator in a random dorm. We were always getting into some mischief. He was intrigued that I wasn't afraid to turn down the dare. He had a nice chocolate complexion, was tall, loved basketball, and had a fraternal twin brother. At first Ryan was sweet, seemed interested in me but shortly after we got to know each other, we began arguing fiercely mostly due to his rude comments. He would irk my nerves like no other, but when we did get along it was an intense connection. It was the epitome of a love hate relationship. It was like when the young boys in elementary pulled your hair because they "liked you". We left the party with make up running down or faces, clothes sticking to our skin, it was the most memorable party we went to that year.

As the semester cruised along, every party we went to I would drink a little more, dance a little longer, and argue with more people, it was wild. Drinking gave me an escape from all the pain in the past. I told myself that I was happy when I was drifting further and further away from my goals and myself. My attitude became ugly and nasty. All the demons that I was suppressing came out when I drank. *Those old wounds won't be able to resonate with your spirit forever, sooner or later you must harness your light and become the person you are destined to be.*

Gary and I began texting and he was adamant about trying to get me alone. I lead him on and never fulfilled the promises to go over to his house. Midterms were approaching but our partying did not slow down one bit. We went out and ran into Ryan and his friends. He and I began to argue and when we were done he shoved me to the side. I was so upset; I left the group and went to the closest party in search of some alcohol. After I drank enough to make me dizzy, I replied to Gary's invite and went to find my friends. Gary wanted me to come over and I agreed. Rain looked me directly in the eyes before I left; she wanted to make sure I really wanted to go. I told her I was fine and that I'd return home soon. I drank the rest of the liquor in my cup and left. Gary lived down the street from us; it was a five-minute walk. The night was cold, breezy, and I had on a black body con dress with brown moccasins.

When I was one block from his apartment, it started raining. He greeted me in the lobby and my drunken mind made him appear more attractive to me. He pulled me in for a long hug and we walked to his place. My heart was thumping and I was fumbling on my words. We went into his bedroom and those old feelings of disgust consumed my body. I ignored it and sat on the bed. Gary began kissing me, and attempted to remove my dress. I felt like I was burning in flames and my thoughts became personified on my skin disguised as sweat. This was not how I pictured my first time to be. I prided myself on waiting almost nineteen years but here I was about to wrap my virginity in silk and give it to this man. *People are nutrients or toxins; be mindful of who you exchange energy with.*

When it was over, I realized I was bleeding and I

rushed to put my underwear back on. Gary must have noticed how concerned I was and asked me what was wrong.

"This was my first time." I said quietly.

"Your first time? Yea ok. What type of virgin comes to a guy house drunk in the middle of the night? Virgin my ass" he snarled.

I pushed him off out of my way and put dress back on. I grabbed his bottle of Sky Vodka off the dresser, slammed the door, and left. I couldn't allow myself to cry because I got myself into the situation. It was done, I made the decision, and I refused to regret it.

As I walked slowly down the dark street, I called Michelle and told her what had just taken place.

"Wow Dez, really? You waited this long for it to happen like this?" she taunted.

"Can you not judge me?" I said softly.

"If you are happy with it then fine." She said.

"Ok I gotta go, talk to you later. Bye" Then I hung up the phone.

I was disappointed by way she responded. I thought she would have reacted differently. I continued to walk and when I got home to my surprise, Ryan was sitting on the bed. His arms were crossed and everyone else was sleep. *What is he doing here? It is 4:00 a.m., why is he still awake?* I thought. He looked me up and down, and got up from the bed.

"Where you been Dezzy?"

"I was at the dorms." I said nervously.

"We just left the dorms an hour ago, whose dorm were you in?"

"Don't worry about it, I was there." I lied.

"You look like you have been drinking; you didn't have sex, did you?" He asked as he walked closer to me.

I walked over to the closet, removed my shoes, and pulled my dress over my head. I was stunned that he asked me that. He somehow knew everything about me.

"Mind your business Ryan!" I snapped.

Ryan was the one I planned on being intimate with but we never got along for more than ten minutes. I felt like I had betrayed him. He looked at me sadly and grabbed my hand.

"What's wrong? Why are you just now getting home?"

"I had a long night, I'm about to shower." I responded as I pulled my hand away from his.

I sat on the toilet and placed my blood-stained underwear on the floor. I cried softly and starred at the pink bathroom rug, I was a complete mess. I pulled my hair into a bun, hopped in the shower and tried to scrub Gary's scent off my skin. After I was done, I put on pajamas and went to bed.

Petal 17

The semester was coming to an end and I was still passing my classes. I was walking home one day when I received a phone call from a number that I did not recognize. I answered, curious to see who it was. After the voice on the other end of the call said hello, I knew exactly who was on the other end of the line.

"Hey." I said.

"How are you?" said India.

"Good." I responded vaguely.

I was not interested in talking to her, I wasn't angry with her, but I did not want to be bothered. The conversation drifted to her being concerned about me going away for college. I was vexed that she was even concerned, I thought why now. We stayed on the phone for around thirty minutes and I found myself sitting on the steps of my apartment laughing and joking with her. It was nice but then I snapped myself out of this happy mood, I wanted answers. *What did she really want? Why did she neglect me my entire life? Why didn't she go to rehab? Why?*

I asked her a series of questions about her behavior and decisions she made when I was younger. She was silent for a few seconds then proceeded to deny everything. She painted herself as an innocent victim. Now I was angry. All the pain from my childhood raced to the forefront on my mind.

"How dare you say you didn't do anything wrong?" You are insane! Don't call me again!" I yelled then clicked the end button on the phone.

I sat on the stairs, my hands were shaking, and my palms were drenched with sweat. She had the audacity to pretend that nothing ever happened. I was hurt and full of rage. That one phone call triggered my actions and mood for the remainder of the second semester. I began drinking more trying to keep the past from gliding back into my mind. I stopped going to class and began to make excuses every Monday. I would go to my professors and get assignments then turn them in online. My main concerns were alcohol and partying.

The following week, my ex from high school, Paul, called me. I was getting ready to go out, guzzling my first drink of the night. He noticed my slurred speech and began questioning me about school and my excessive drinking. We kept in touch through text messages so he knew my party schedule well. He continued to preach to me about the importance of staying focused on my classes and my responses were full of eye rolls and denial. We began arguing. I did not want to hear any of it; I felt judged. He was disappointed and I was livid. We hung up and didn't speak to each other for years. He tried to save me from self- destruction. *When we hurt, our tribe hurts. When we heal, our tribe heals. This is bigger than you.*

I spiraled and everything around me crumbled. My

friendship with my roommates diminished, I felt like everyone was against me. After the experience with Gary, I did not want to have sex ever again. I continued to drink, not realizing the power it had over me. I truly felt alone, depressed, and extremely low. I had to deal with the betrayal of my drug addict mother, neglect from my friends, and the reality of a father who failed to restore my faith in men. I hated it all.

One Saturday night, I wondered away alone from a party. I was intoxicated and stumbled onto the stairs of our apartment. I sat there, screaming, crying, wanting it all to be over with. I convinced myself that I was done with living, done with the pain, done with trying and failing. I dialed Michelle's number, she answered and I took a huge breath.

"Hey girl, I just wanted to tell you I love you and thank you for everything." I said in between sniffles.

"What's wrong? You are scaring me." She asked concerned.

"I don't want to be alive anymore, it hurts too much." I said as I cried.

"Dezari, do not talk like that. I swear if you kill yourself, I'm killing myself too, we can't live without each other." She said.

Her words shot through me like bullets. I wanted her to continue to live a happy, healthy, blissful life. I wanted her to achieve every dream and conquer everything that I couldn't. I wanted peace and told myself that death was the only way to get it. I fantasied about how I wouldn't have to feel any more sorrow. After hearing those words from Michelle, I told myself to hold on. She was the most important person to me, more than a cousin, more than a sister, and more than a friend.

She was the only reason I didn't end it all.

We sat on the phone crying together. She stayed on the phone with me and began to tell me every reason that I had to live. I was finally able to pick up my broken, intoxicated body off the stairs. I walked into my bedroom, sat on the floor, and texted Angela. The text read "I can't live out here anymore, I won't make it."

Angela didn't ask why or try to persuade me to stay at the university that I worked so hard to get into. She did exactly what I needed her to do; she listened. She replied, "Ok move out here with me, I'll send you a ticket at the end of the summer."

I read her text and got in the bed. I told myself to fight the same way I'd always fought. I had to fight for myself, for my sanity, my happiness, my peace, I told myself to fight for it all. *You have the power to transform any situation; you are the conjurer.*

After the semester was over, I moved back to the Bay Area. Most of my family criticized my decision for leaving Northridge and I didn't care. I knew a change had to be made.

As promised Angela sent me a plane ticket in the beginning of August. I was heavy, full of baggage but hopeful. I promised myself that I would heal and make this a new beginning.

I boarded the plane and sat in the window seat. I looked outside the window and watched the men hurrying to board the luggage. I imagined how my life would be in a new state, then I prayed and asked for things to get better. I nestled into my seat and looked to my right and saw a young girl in the aisle across from me. She was wearing a sunflower backpack; I blinked several times to confirm what I saw. A wave of peace came over me and I acknowledged the light and protection around me. I was exactly where I was meant to be. I closed my eyes, leaned my curly head against the window, and told myself...*time to blossom.*

I emailed this letter to my father 3/29/14. Although I didn't receive a response, the letter served its purpose. It was the fertilizer for this book and the beginning of my healing journey. (Excuse the typos and grammatical errors)

Dear Dad,

This letter was not written to shame you or make you feel less of a man, it was written so that I can free emotions that I've been holding onto for years. I cried while writing this entire letter. I cried for the teenage girl inside of me that was afraid to cry. First off, I love you, I love you more than I can put into words. Being your first child, I was your test dummy, you definitely didn't know how to raise a daughter & I can't punish or blame you for that. The way that a woman allows a man to treat her is all based on her relationship with her father. Our relationship has been rocky and covered up with the glory of you being a single father. I just want you to know how I felt growing up. Waking up that night to you touching my breast confused the hell out of me. I immediately thought how could my best friend betray me? I hated myself, I hated my body, all because I blamed the two for breaking our bond. After that night, I haven't really trusted you. Again I don't want you to feel as if I'm writing this letter to hurt you, I'm writing this letter to heal myself. Moving onto the time you actually had the audacity to lick my nipple, I again felt disgusted with myself. I asked myself why did God give me two parents who couldn't seem to get it right. Already struggling with accepting my skin tone & body shape, YOU yes you made me want to run far away from myself. Over the years your mistakes continued but I never hated you for them. I always told myself that you had problems that you needed to workout with God. Today, I have learned to love & accept my body. I love the woman that I'm becoming, I love everything about myself. I want to thank you for making your mistakes because in the end they molded me into a queen. When I'm blessed with children of my own, I doubt that you will be allowed to be in the same room as them without my presence. Because of you I'm going to be a better mother, wife, and woman. Thank you for mistakes, they molded me into a queen.

About the Author

Dezari is an author and poet currently residing on the west coast. She uses her platform VibestoBlossom.com to encourage holistic healthy living. She believes that once you heal yourself, you heal those who came before you and those who are yet to come. Visit the website for healing tools and contact information. As always, she's wishing you love and light.

Keep blossoming!!

Made in the USA
Columbia, SC
23 October 2017